BLESSED ARE THE MEEK

BLESSED ARE THE MEEK

A CASE FOR HUMILITY IN A TIME OF ARROGANCE

DR. JOHN MONACO

Commonwealth Books Inc.,

CONTENTS

Dedication vii

    1

    3

    5

    7

1

    8

    20

2

    21

    32

3

    33

4

    51

    60

5

    61

    74

vi - CONTENTS

6

                                    75

7

                                    90

8

                                   104

                                   118

9

                                   119

                                   129

DEDICATION

To my Lisa, my source and my light.

A Commonwealth Publications Paperback
BLESSED ARE THE MEEK:
A CASE FOR HUMILITY IN A TIME OF ARROGANCE:
SURVIVING TRUMP AND CORONAVIRUS
This edition published 2021
by Commonwealth Books
All rights reserved

Copyright © 2021 by John Monaco
Published in the United States by Commonwealth Books Inc., New York.

Library of Congress Control Number: 2021930999

ISBN: 978-1-892986-24-5

No part of this book may be reproduced or utilized in any form or by any means, electronic or mechanical, including photocopying, recording, or by any information storage retrieval system, without permission in writing from the publisher, except by a reviewer who may quote brief passages in a review to be printed in a newspaper, magazine or journal.

This work is a self-help book and there are actual person (s) or events or similarities to events possibly contained.

First Commonwealth Books Trade Edition: April 2021

PUBLISHED BY COMMONWEALTH BOOKS, INC.,
www.commonwealthbooks@aol.com
www.commonwealthbooksinc.com

Manufactured in the United States of America

**BLESSED ARE THE MEEK:
A CASE FOR HUMILITY IN A TIME OF ARROGANCE:
SURVIVING TRUMP AND CORONAVIRUS**

John E. Monaco, MD

Commonwealth Books Inc.,
New York 2021

2 - DR. JOHN MONACO

Author's Note

The gestation period for this book occurred during 2016-2020, one of the most-tumultuous periods in history. The conceptualization of the humility over arrogance paradigm came to a climax during the height of the Covid-19 pandemic during the first half of 2020. During this period of personal and societal angst, I theorized that our society was plagued by a culture of arrogance, the antidote of which may be humility, as exemplified by the beatitude: "Blessed are the meek, for they shall inherit the earth."

The trends toward autocracy, the mismanagement of the early stages of the pandemic, the crisis at the southern border, as well as the current challenges of the health-care system, personal wealth and personal well-being were, in my view, examples of our arrogant culture characterized by the dual epidemics of loneliness and disconnection. I attempted to make the case that humility, or meekness, may in fact be the basic human value that might serve us better during these, and ANY times.

Much happened after the initial manuscript was accepted for publication: Trump lost to Biden in decisive, yet disputed (for some) manner, nearly 600,000 souls perished to Covid 19, a virus whose very existence is questioned by a stubbornly persistent segment of the population, racial tensions reached a new height with the murders of George Floyd and Breonna Taylor during the spring and summer of 2020, putting into common usage terms like "wokeness" and "cancel culture", the U.S. Capitol was attacked by insurrectionists wishing to overturn the results of the 2020 election, egged on by President Trump to do so, mask wearing, social distancing and vaccine availability and administration became political issues and the entire world faced the possibility of economic collapse due to the pandemic. And don't forget the threats to the planet by global climate change, worldwide immigration and refugee crises, and the challenges of the world food supply and nutrition. And, as they say in the old infomercials, "That's not all!"

In this author's view, these events simply reinforced the point of view of this book. Had we, as individuals and as a society embraced the inclusiveness and openness of humility over the disconnection and alienation of arrogance, all of us would be in a healthier, and possibly happier place.

My wish and my prayer is that the power of meekness presented two thousand years ago, abide in us today, and for the next two thousand years, so that we may inherit the earth.

INTRODUCTION

I awoke from a sound sleep, gasping, in a cold sweat, and wracked with anxiety. Was I having another heart attack? Did I just have a frightening dream? Was I dying?

That was fairly common for me. My propensity for that kind of physical reaction to emotional distress probably explained my need for open-heart surgery and coronary-bypass grafting relatively early in life at the age of fifty-six. The fight-or-flight response to stress make the body react with physiology that can save us in times of perceived danger by giving us acuity of thought, muscle contraction, shrinking blood flow to the extremities, and an increase in heart rate and blood pressure. If chronic and recurring frequently, however, these physiologic responses will eventually kill us.

I needed to mitigate my stress response. My heart was pounding, and I had the usual dull headache of high blood pressure. I tried to distract myself from the cause of my anxiety by thinking about other things, trying to focus on the book I'd been trying to write for years. I submitted several manuscripts for it, but none were accepted.

My working title was *Blessed Are the Meek: A Case for Humility*. I still thought it was reasonable concept with potential for wide reader interest, so why couldn't I get someone interested in publishing it?

I have been told I'm at my best when teaching, lecturing, or trying to make an important point to a group or individual by telling stories, anecdotes, and recounting my history.

An idea struck like a lightning bolt. I would start the book over, and I would begin by telling the story of how we were caught up in the hysteria surrounding Hurricane Irma impacting Florida, my state, in 2017. That landfall and devastation coincided with the death of my eighty-eight-year-old father of Parkinson's disease, bladder cancer, and heart and kidney failure.

As I lay in bed, it occurred to me, while trying not to think about my worries of children, work, my aging widowed mother, my wife's horrible divorce from her abusive ex-husband, repairs for the car and house, my health, and the state of our country and the world, that the events of that September weekend in 2017 illustrated many of the points I tried to make in writing *Blessed Are the Meek* (BATM).

I share that story to illustrate the organic nature from which this book evolved, hoping it will enrich the reader's appreciation of the stories and points I will try to give. It forms the point of the entire book.

If someone is reading this, that means I was able to convince a publisher to take a chance on a book idea that germinated in me for most of a decade, through many life changes and adventures that reinforced my initial feeling that eventually became my life philosophy. The meek *are* indeed blessed, and they *shall* inherit the earth.

PART ONE

THE HUMILITY/ARROGANCE INTERFACE: STATING THE PROBLEM

CHAPTER 1

Meekness?

As I lay awake that night, worried about everything I could think of. I reflected again on what had become an obsessive idea. Surprisingly, it was one of the Beatitudes, the blessings spoken by Jesus as depicted in Matthew in the famous Sermon on the Mount.

The one that stuck in my head was, *Blessed are the meek, for they shall inherit the earth.* No matter how hard I tried, I couldn't get those words out of my mind. Later, I came to realize this seemingly intrusive thought was God and the universe speaking to me. It was my mission to make sense of that beatitude, to teach it, and to use it to benefit all.

The only problem was, it ran counter to everything people knew about success, especially in America with Trump as president. He won by saying Americans had to be winners again, to be better than the rest of the world and to exclude everyone else.

That seemed like the exact opposite of meekness. I came to realize it was precisely the opposite, which explained why his approach kept failing.

I fell asleep before making any headway, so at least my immediate mission was accomplished. I defeated my insomnia by clearing my mind of worries. However, I did it by replacing those with an obsessive thought that was so intrusive, it remained with me when I awoke the following morning.

I awoke, as usual, before anyone else in the house. After my morning thoughts and meditation, I walked my beloved dog, Snickers, and decided to delve more deeply into the thought that obsessed me. I started by defining the terms. What did meekness mean? Was it the same thing it meant 2,000 years earlier?

I looked up synonyms for meek. The primary ones were tame, spiritless, modest, humble....

Humble! That's it! I thought.

Meekness had to refer to humility, which wasn't the same as tame or spiritless. Being humble actually required nonboastful strength, confidence, and knowing who you were without big demonstrations of one's strength or prowess.

The opposite of meekness was arrogance. I felt I was finally getting somewhere. Perhaps the beatitude meant, *By being humble and rejecting arrogance, there is a reward, something that equates to inheriting the earth.*

That had to be positive. I wasn't quite there, but I was close, and the nagging voice in my head admonished me to get to the bottom of that millennia-old conundrum.

I began thinking about attachment behavior and connectedness vs. separation. Maybe the answer lay somewhere in that conceptual swamp.

Brene Brown wrote that the two strongest drives for humans are love and belonging. Belonging is another way of saying attachment, the instinctual drive for humans to be connected. Psychologist John Bowlby first described the need of attachment to a primary caregiver in infants. The theory later was applied to adult relationships. When a relationship functions well, the individuals within it exhibit secure attachment behavior. When it isn't functioning, their attachment becomes anxious, ambivalent, or disorganized.

Without digressing too far, that means we all strive to be attached. I will discuss that topic later in the book. First, we must feel lovable and worthy, although even a sense of self-worth requires a certain degree of humility.

For the moment, I accepted that we all had an internal, instinctual drive to be attached to others. When we are attached, we are stronger as a people, more joyful, and more successful in life. Not to put too much into the movie *Jerry McGuire* as an accurate description of human behavior, I wondered if it could be that we could only say honestly, "You complete me," once we were successfully attached to another human being?

My contention is that we must strive toward humility or meekness to connect successfully with others. Why? Humility requires empathy, the ability to see the world or feel its effects through the experiences of another.

Humility requires that we see all people as basically the same. This may make many people shiver in discomfort, because we have been driven by cultural programming that humans are stratified, with some being more qualified than others to feel worthy. The truth is, all people in the world are driven by the same fundamental needs. At a very basic level, people need to be safe, fed, warm, dry, and not under attack.

Painting human needs with a broader stroke, it is clear that once basic needs are met, there is also a need to be connected. All people strive for love and belonging (connection). We face the same fears, with death and rejection the most fundamental.

That is where humility comes in. We *all* have the same basic needs and are plagued by the same basic fears. Meekness dictates that we recognize that all human beings share those characteristics. The opposite of meekness is arrogance, which dictates that individuals have fundamental differences in their needs and basic human characteristics. When we feel there are fundamental differences between people, we can't help embracing the concept of the "other." When we see each other as different, it's human nature to become apprehensive and inevitably fearful of the other. Fear leads to hatred, conflict, and extreme separation.

Could it be that the beatitude wished to express that by being meeker, or humbler, we would see the similarities between all humans. In so doing, we could connect. Taken to its logical conclusion, we would become part of the entire family of man. We would then inherit the earth.

Here is the beatitude, followed by a restatement using my chosen synonyms and deeper meanings.

> Blessed are the meek, for they shall inherit the earth.
>
> Blessed are the humble, for they shall connect with their fellow man and become one with the universe of mankind, understanding each other and feeling empathy toward our fellow man.
>
> Blessed are those who can love, for they shall be connected.

This can be examined from a more-practical perspective by looking at well-known individuals.

At the humble end of the spectrum, there are people like the prophets—Jesus, Buddha, Mohammed—and those who have sacrificed to better the lives of the disadvantaged, the poor, and the sick, such as Mother Theresa, Gandhi, and Dr. Martin Luther King, Jr. These individuals possessed the humility to recognize that humans are, in fact, connected to each other and the entirety of humanity. They did it by realizing and teaching that it is our duty as human beings to treat individuals with love, care, compassion, and empathy. That requires humility and no arrogance. It results in connection. Through that, these remarkable individuals actually inherited the earth. They made the world and they people they met better.

To emphasize that point further, their lives made it clear that the opposite of humility is arrogance. Intrinsic within arrogance is the requirement that we treat all other people as different and remain separate from them.

That shows how humility leads to connection, while arrogance results in separation. Connection results in strength, love, and improvement of the human condition. Separation results in a weakening and worsening of the human condition. Worst of all, separation, as a result of arrogance, results in fear of others, which leads to hate.

There are also examples of those who live arrogant lives and embrace separation, fear, and hate. The most poignant example is President Donald J. Trump.

I would like to explore how his living arrogantly, counter to the beatitude that instructs us to live humbly, has gotten him where he is. His philosophy of life has worked beautifully for him, but it has had devastating results for the rest of us.

The Trump Conundrum

D-Day 2019 was the seventy-fifth anniversary of perhaps the most-important day of the twenty-first century. That day marked the end of the quintessential conflict of modern times, when the causes of compassion and liberty that were embraced by the Western democracies of the world, chose to rid the world of a truly monstrous ideology and a murderous dictator intent on complete, horrific ethnic cleansing.

The issues were clear. For most of the world, that invasion and its ensuing battles were a clear example of good vs. evil, the forces of light vs. the forces of darkness. It was a conflict of truly biblical proportions.

President Trump visited Normandy to celebrate the heroism of that day. He gave speeches, placed wreaths, and acknowledged surviving heroes and widows. While he spoke in eloquent, respectful tones, in the background, he was his usual arrogant self. In his off time, he tweeted about the Mueller investigation, made references to crooked Hillary, and threatened to levy tariffs on Mexico if that country refused to comply with his immigration-restriction demands.

Based on my arrogance vs. humility model, I have figured Trump out. No matter where someone stands on the political/philosophical spectrum, I feel my thesis makes sense.

To understand how Trump works, one needs to consider several basic facts. One—whatever the topic is, it's about him. He's the center of the universe, and the world revolves around him. Two—he is arrogant.

Given my paradigm, that means he feels no true connection to other human beings and is certain he is superior to most. He is grandiose and obscenely self-confident. He is a man who reads no briefing reports, barely arrives in the Oval Office before noon, and make pronouncements and major policy decisions based on opinions found on Fox News, which he watches constantly during his "executive time." As Senator Klobucher said in the first debate, "Important policy decisions should not be made at five AM in your bathrobe."

His arrogance results in a complete lack of empathy. How else could he stomach the horrible treatment given to children separated from their parents at the border? All he said in response to that was, "It was worse under Obama, way worse." That, of course, was a complete lie.

His lack of humility, extreme arrogance, and inability to feel anyone else's pain results in every interaction with another person being transactional. Worse, he doesn't just view people as winners or losers. He thinks there are only winners and suckers. Every interaction and the way he runs his presidency bears an uncanny resemblance to an episode of *The Apprentice*.

Seen through that lens, Donald Trump's behavior makes sense—or, at least, it can be rationally explained.

Despots he gets along with are considered "nice" or write "excellent letters" propping up Trump's ego. Most individuals on the planet are inferior or dangerous. The most obvious example of that are the people who cross into the U.S. via the southern border, who he terms rapists, murderers, felons, and drug smugglers.

What can be learned from the arrogance of such a man? His policies have resulted in children being abandoned at the southern border, suffering while he celebrated the Fourth of July by giving himself a parade. Have Americans ever been exposed to such a display of ego?

Maybe that's where the lesson is. Americans can only hope Trump's repellant arrogance and its divisiveness don't tear the country apart before he's voted out of office or removed by legal or legislative means. His actions are important in demonstrating to us the opposite pole of humility and how much more successful that is in forming connections.

The problem is, Trump doesn't want connection except to people who agree with him. He and his followers seek division, a clear demarcation of us and them. Them become the others—immigrants, Democrats, brown people, and even women, as evidence by his saying, "They let you grab their pussies when you're famous."

The lesson from this is that sometimes, arrogance is proscribed as a road map to gaining power. Division sometimes succeeds. Humans operate with a mixture of arrogance and humility. The beatitude teaches us to lead a satisfying, complete, and happy life, we should trend toward humility and meekness in our interactions with others.

Trump, unlike most people, is almost completely arrogant. Leaders like Dr. King and Nelson Mandela trend toward humble in their interactions, teachings, and the way they live their lives. This results in connection and attracts other people to follow out of love, not for hate of the other like Trumpists.

What does it mean for those who want to live their lives in a meaningful, loving way? Even if we have aspirations for public office, we still need to lay the foundation for a loving life. That is a baseline assumption.

This beatitude, with its admonition to lead a humble, meek life, is relevant to almost every aspect of our lives, from personal relationships to professional lives to artistic endeavors and the way we handle our finances and approach our artistic, aesthetic lives.

This book explores ways that our approach to this beatitude affects the complexion of ours lives and what we can do to lead a more-meaningful, loving, giving life. That strikes me as the point of being on earth.

Let us learn ways to find the strength and perspective to change in positive ways to create more-successful, meaningful lives.

Personal Relationships

How do we use the apparent duality between humility and arrogance? As I pointed out in *From Duality to Unity* (1968), when it comes to human emotion, what appears to be duality is actually unity. We use the combination of emotions to best benefit our goals. That may sound confusing, so I'll explain.

As pointed out concerning Trump and most other leaders, we exist as a mosaic of arrogance and humility. The beatitude blesses us to lean toward humility, because that's best for our souls and for humanity. There are times, though, like during the fight-or-flight response when we're in danger, where a dose of arrogance could prove self-protective and may give us the confidence of leaders. Without the balance of humility, even that kind of arrogance can be damaging to humanity.

Human relationships are the same. A humble acceptance of another person's life experience is important for a successful relationship, while a modicum of occasional arrogance is required for survival. People love confident partners, but it's more important to be compassionate, understanding, and empathic—that is, humble. In times of conflict in a relationship, the more-successful virtue is humbly, meekly to accept the shared humanity of one's partner. Confidence is good, but kindness always triumphs in times of stress.

Unity combines the duality of arrogance and humility such that either one is accessible depending on the needs of the situation. The beatitude teaches us that if given the choice, leaning toward humility is the compassionate, loving, unifying approach.

Another aspect of Trump that serves as a wonderful teaching moment for the application of *Blessed are the meek* is the humility to face reality about yourself and others' observations of you. Long before his candidacy, Trump showed that he loves, accepts, and assists those who admire him and shower him with compliments, deserved or not. As of this writing, the British ambassador has been banned from the White House for having the audacity to discuss the chaos and ineptitude of the current White House. Trump proclaimed that was fake, but people know it's true.

A humble person would accept such criticism, discuss its veracity with the person who expressed those things, and maybe take time for a little self-reflection that someone observed deficiencies in the operation and values of the current administration. The humble accept criticism as an opportunity for improvement. The arrogant receive criticism as disloyalty, which is punishable by banishment or other penalty.

Let's look at some more everyday practical ways we can utilize an inclination toward humility to better our lives, relationships, and society in general.

There's no question that one of the major characteristics of arrogance is a sense of moral superiority. In that person's eyes, his decision-making is exceptional. Those who aren't competent to handle difficult moral decisions, like how to handle kids seeking asylum at the southern border, will reply that the cruelty and inhumanity isn't as bad as it seems, or it's someone else's responsibility. It's almost as if the person knows his decisions are morally wrong but is still able to avoid all responsibility.

When Trump was asked why he allowed a crowd of supporters to chant, "Send her back," referring to the brown-skinned freshman Congressman Omar, Trump said he tried to stop it by moving to a different topic. A review of the recording showed that is an outright lie.

The arrogant lie easily to protect their images. They don't have the courage or self-awareness to accept their true selves nor to divulge them to those close to them or who support them.

Lies, deflection, placing blame, not accepting blame, and even violence to anyone who comes close to exposing an arrogant person's true self are all ready weapons. Many such individuals are abusive in their relationships and on the world stage, because they can't accept the responsibility of being exposed for who they really are. They create an illusion about themselves to achieve their goal. The arrogant believe only in winners and suckers. They won't suffer losers. If they have to, they will destroy them or completely humiliate them, turning them into suckers.

I knew an abusive man who, after years of psychological, sexual, and physical abuse at his hands, saw his wife of twenty years take their children and leave for their own safety. He was the epitome of arrogance. Not only did he feel he didn't need any other human beings for his existence, he felt he was better than everyone else. To succeed in life, he not only had to beat his adversaries. He had to humiliate and annihilate them.

The primary subject of his abuse was his wife, for whom he held disdain for reasons only his therapist or God would know. Being a physician, she led a fulfilling, meaningful life that he didn't understand except to the degree that it improved his standing in the community and his reputation to be married to a doctor.

The abuser, the ultimate narcissist, lacked empathy and, therefore, humility. Like Trump, who may also be abusive, he was the ultimate example of arrogance. He lacked the meekness to ever connect honestly with another human being. To him, relationships were about power, control, and self-aggrandizement. When the object of an abuser steps out of line, making him look bad or making him lose control or power, that person is abused, humiliated, and punished until he or she is reined back into line.

An abuser, as an ultimate arrogant individual, insists on activity to fill the day, not understanding the concept of dynamism or any activity that is meaningful, enriching, and healing to the world. His mind must be kept occupied, because without empathy or humility, he lacks any capacity for worry, concern, guilt, or stress. If he doesn't feel, he never hurts, yet he is incredibly capable of unleashing hurt on others to make himself feel more powerful. All interactions are contests, and the arrogant person must win every time.

That individual, whom I will call Dick, had a lifelong history of antisocial behavior. He was incapable of forming interpersonal relationships based on trust and love. He had plenty of relationships, but they were based on mutual self-interest or shared tasks.

He married a younger woman who always felt there was something off about him, but she felt she was just being overly cautious about marrying an older man she barely knew. He carefully calculated the whole situation. His fiancée was young, beautiful, smart, and training to become a doctor, which made him look better. He won by getting her.

The abuse began soon after they married. He exerted power and control almost immediately. To him, that was a relationship. His arrogance disallowed him from any human connection. What he interpreted as connection meant control, power, and all decision making of anything financial.

His new wife was a humble, empathic person, the kind the beatitude would describe as meek. She connected with everyone she met—work mates, patients, neighbors, friends, relatives, and eventually their children, with whom she bonded completely. They were the central force in her life.

Dick never liked the children. They took his wife's time and energy that was supposed to be devoted to him. He eventually abused them, too. Some of it was the usual thing, like slapping, degrading, or isolating them in their rooms. Other parts were downright sinister, in keeping with his military training. Some things were so bizarre and cruel that law-enforcement officials could barely believe he did them.

One of his favorite techniques he called "gaslighting," based on a suspense thriller of the mid-twentieth century, where home gaslight strength was reduced each night secretly by an abuser to make the victims think they were losing their minds.

Dick's method was even more insidious. He hid things from family members, like car keys or greeting cards purchased for family and friends' holidays. When the family members searched for those items, Dick said he had no idea where they were. Slowly, his wife and kids began to think they were going crazy.

When the abuse reached a particularly diabolical and dangerous point, especially for the youngest child, his son and his favorite, his wife decided it was time to leave. She moved her possessions and children to an apartment away from her husband.

He immediately became even more vindictive, angry, and mean. His arrogance couldn't handle the fact that his wife had the nerve to take his children from him. He sued for divorce, accusing her of abandonment, and he gained custody of the children by claiming she alienated the children from him, which was an absurd, baseless accusation designed to take the spotlight off his years of abuse and neglect.

Once again, because of his arrogance and complete inability to see the situation through his loved ones' lives, he continued winning, always staying in the paradigm of winners and suckers.

In the end, ironically, he lost. His children weren't fooled by his accusation about his ex-wife. Once they reached eighteen, they immediately moved out of his home and in with their mother. They planned never to include him in their lives again.

That was an extreme case of arrogance that resulted in separation and disconnection. Meekness leads to connection and belonging. Arrogance leads to separation, abandonment, and disconnection. He chose the arrogant path. His personality wouldn't allow him to do otherwise, and he ended up childless and alone. Had he been humbler, exhibiting more empathy and self-examination, he might still have his children in his life despite the collapse of his marriage. His path, however, led him to darkness.

The comparisons of an arrogant sociopath to our current president are astounding. Their approach to other people is characterized by a complete lack of empathy. Both are unable to see anyone else's life but their own. The actions of others are impotent when it comes to affecting those men.

This shows the distinction between arrogance and humility and how humility is synonymous with meekness, which leads to connection, allowing the meek to inherit the earth. Arrogant individuals, like Dick and Trump, exclude disconnect, fear, and hate. They will leave the earth completely separated from it, alienating all those who attempt to get close.

I will leave those two for the moment and focus on how we can live more humbly and why that is so important for the survival of ourselves, the planet, and our relationships with others. What follows is the story of a remarkable young lady.

PART TWO

FOSTERING HUMILITY
HUMBLE HERO

CHAPTER 2

Dick's daughter put up with years of emotional abuse—gaslighting, usurping her power, and squelching her individuality. Based on that, she should have emerged with a desperate, negative outlook, but she didn't. Through it all, she never became negative.

She is one of the most-moving examples of the triumph of humility over arrogance I have ever known. Because of that, I have no doubt she will someday inherit the earth.

When she moved out of his home at the age of eighteen, he completely cut off contact, refusing to pay for college or anything else in her life. Dick told his ex-wife that he would reconsider his position if she came to his house and spoke with him.

When she graduated from high school, that angry, abusive man, angry over the disrespect his adult daughter showed him, set up a post-graduation dinner with his friends. He emailed her about it, expecting her to attend and pay him the respect he deserved.

She spent most of her graduation fielding his abusive, ridiculing texts and emails and decided it wasn't worth it to spend such an important day in her life in his presence. Any mental health counselor or therapist would support such a position. Based on the history of abuse she received from Dick, they would have advised her to avoid him. His only intention would be to demean and humiliate her, even on her graduation day.

When the day passed, however, she felt guilty. She had a conscience and a sense of empathy, something completely lacking in her father. She told her friend, "Maybe I should have gone to his dinner, but he was so awful to me that day, I couldn't bring myself to face him."

They agreed with her, saying she should take care of herself.

"Still," she said, "I feel bad for him."

"Are you kidding me?" her best friend asked. "As awful as he's been to you, you still feel bad for him?"

The young lady had a heart. She was humble and knew that all people are connected no matter how disconnected they may feel from time-to-time. She understood that we are in the presence of a power greater than ourselves, the main purpose of which is to maintain that connection and support it with love and compassion.

Because of her ability to be so meek and humble, she will always be connected to the others in her universe. By maintaining that connection, she will someday inherit the earth.

Kindness—An Outdated Concept?

We have struggled to clarify what it means to be humble and meek and how, in the modern world, we can adapt that beatitude that admonishes us to be meek, to lead a more-meaningful, engaged, connected life. This makes us feel as if we have inherited or become one with the earth.

I know a man I'll call Chuck, who takes the concept of kindliness to the point of saintliness. The way he lives his life illustrates my point.

Chuck is a ballroom dance instructor, but that's far from all he does. In every aspect of his life, he is kind. It shows in the way he teachers, the manner in which he interacts with his fellow professionals, his dedication to being a safety professional in our local running race community, where we take part in races like Disney marathons.

One night on his way home from the dance studio, he stayed late after an evening group lesson so he could meet with the studio owner. As he drove home in a rush, hoping to spend some quality time with his wife, he came upon flashing lights and saw there was an emergency. He was horrified to see a car on fire.

Having worked in the emergency-response industry, he carried some flares in his car. The policeman was having trouble directing the busy rush hour traffic around the crash site, so Chuck got out of his car, placed a couple of strategic flares to point the way for anxious motorists, and began assisting the officer with the traffic flow just when drivers were losing patience and getting testy.

Chuck stayed to help until the power company could arrive and cut the downed power lines and the EMS team dealt with the injured passengers. Once the fire department extinguished the car fire, and tow trucks cleared away the wreckage, Chuck felt it was safe to leave.

He told the supervising officer he was leaving, and that poised, authoritarian man gave him a big hug and said, "Thank you, Man." He looked at Chuck more closely. "Weren't you the guy who picked up our check at the restaurant the other night?"

He was. Once he acknowledged it, the officer hugged him a second time.

That is the nature of kindness, reaching out to help another even when it isn't needed, without any expectation of reward or recognition. Kindness is the clearest example of the human connection that comes with humility.

There was recently a great hubbub when Ellen Degeneres sat next to ex-President George W. Bush at a sporting event. They come from opposite ends of the political spectrum and disagree on significant topics.

As Ellen says, "When I talk about there needs to be more kindness in the way we treat each other, I mean we need to have kindness for everyone, whether we agree with them or not."

Such is the essence of the importance of kindness as the ultimate humble connector we should embrace.

Leadership

In these arrogant Trumpian times, we are taught a leader must be strong, a winner, authoritarian, and, therefore, arrogant. Meekness or humility are signs of weakness and make terrible leaders.

I maintain the opposite. The best leaders are the humble ones. They should be the ones we follow after Trump.

Trump leads by threatening adversaries with destruction, humiliation, or profound regret. Sometimes that works, but only by isolating, disconnecting, and driving away. Allegiances become impossible to form, and trust is lost. No one wins.

Both sides can only claim they'll no longer have a relationship with the other to avoid feeling threatened. Nothing productive comes from such an adversarial approach. Success in the international realm is nothing more than successful leadership on the world stage.

Anyone in the military, industry, a large family, or a hospital setting like the places I worked for decades knows that successful leaders, the ones who get their people working together as a cohesive team to accomplish productive goals, lead by following one central principle: "I, as a leader, won't ask those under me to do anything I won't do myself."

That is leadership by example, where the leader recognizes the identities of those he or she leads. When those being led are treated humbly by interacting with them, allowing them to feel they are noticed, understood, and recognized for having needs other than those the leader has, then those people will feel more connected with the leader. Goals become more-efficiently accomplished. The leader and the led feel more successful, as if they accomplished something relevant.

I have always been a huge fan of the movie *White Christmas*. An important plot line in that popular holiday film is the adoration that Danny Kaye and Bing Crosby characters have for their former World War Two General Waverley. They come to his aid by resurrecting the popularity of the Vermont inn that the general runs in his retirement.

While discussing how important and beloved the general was by his men, Bing Crosby said, "First we ate, then he ate. First we slept, then he slept."

Eventually, they reunited their old company for a Christmas Eve/General Waverley birthday celebration. Before their moving rendition of the title song, *White Christmas*, the men sing, *We'll Follow the Old Man Wherever He Wants to Lead*. Not only do they respect his title as their leader, they recognize him as a fellow man with same post-war needs they face. His leadership style involved being one of them, and the power of that style paid off in terms of connection and giving value and relevance to his life.

As a sports fan, I feel a particular fondness for coaches and managers who are former players, because they understand the rigorous practice and game schedule the players face. My home team, the Tamps Bay Rays, describe their manager or "skipper" as "one of the boys." He understands them, sees them, and they know they are noticed and matter. For that reason, they go deep into the playoffs each year. The best leaders lead from within, as one of the guys. They see each other and give each other relevance. They will inherit the earth. Someday, the Rays might win the World Series.

Marriage and Relationships

Many men in long-term marriages say, "It's far better to be happy than right." So much of marital conflict, or in any conflict between human beings, comes from the desire to be right. Sometimes, the frustration to be right results in seeing who can shout the loudest.

I'm married to my third wife and can't claim to be a marriage counselor, but I have learned a few things about how to get along without compromising the essence of yourself and what you need from a relationship and life.

I've had my share of arguments in a marital relationship. In each of them, there is a similar pattern. An accusation is made, typically over some slight, oversight, or even betrayal. The hurt party makes this accusation known by reciting his or her version of how it happened, explaining what the offending party did or didn't do. It takes the form of a presentation of facts that amount to a story told from the hurt party's point of view. Whether those facts represent the truth is a matter of opinion. The dispute over that truth becomes the crux of the discussion. The other party presents his or her side, which seems entirely different from what the first party said.

As an example, Bob and Judy, in their late thirties or early forties, have been married for almost ten years. They have two kids around school age. They are middle class to upper middle class and are comfortable economically, with a nice suburban house. Bob works in an office in a nearby large city, commuting to work each day. Judy stays home to care for the kids and the home. By all accounts, they have a happy marriage and idyllic family.

One day, Bob had lunch with a female client. A neighbor saw them at the restaurant, and that person felt the need to report the meeting to Judy. In the report, the person said repeatedly, "I didn't see anything happen," but the person added, "They left in the same car. Bob held the door for her."

In truth, she was a business client, and it was a truly innocent meeting.

Judy assumed it was a potential love interest of Bob's. Perhaps, in the worst-case scenario, they were in the early stages of an affair.

When confronted with that possibility, Bob, rather than seeing her point of view and gently, honestly allaying her anxieties, jumped immediately to defiance. He accused her of not trusting him and wondered if she might be the one who was cheating, since she jumped to that conclusion so quickly.

Either way, both chose the arrogant path of separation from the mindset and experience of the other, moving immediately to fear, which always leads to resentment and hate.

The humble approach in marriages and relationships is for each partner not only to be loving and trusting but to try to see a scenario from the other person's point of view. That is connection. The arrogant approach fosters disconnection and resentment. It requires open communication that is possibly only through cultivated trust. That is the humble way of dealing with marital conflict, which is much more likely to foster connection.

Parenting

One of the most challenging yet rewarding experiences of being human is to raise children. It might be difficult to see why there is a need to decide whether the humble or arrogant approach is best. The mistake most people make is that they think the humble approach to parenting doesn't account for the need for discipline.

The distinctions can be better understood by examining the difference between authoritarian and authoritative parenting. The authoritative parent can be humbly by asserting they are in charge and have the ultimate say over the rules and how they are enforced. That position is held by virtue of their age, experience, and intrinsic respect as parents.

The authoritarian parent rules with the proverbial iron fist, invoking extreme punishment if the child doesn't obey all the parent's directives. Such a parent sees no connection between his or her experience and that of the child. For the extremely arrogant authoritarian parent, children aren't even part of the same species. It's difficult for empathy to take hold in that scenario, and the child ends up fearing the parent, always worrying about getting into trouble and never feeling as if he is truly being seen.

The humble, authoritative parent earns respect rather than demands it. The child has no doubt who is in charge in the family, and that it's the parent's role to raise the child, but that relationship is based on mutual respect. There is humility in both directions, as neither party sees themselves as better or worse, just fellow human beings with different roles in the family. There's no arrogant separation, only humble connection and attachment, and, dare I say it, love?

Authoritarian parents, like authoritarian leaders, rule out of fear. Children of such parents are rarely secure and often feel extremely anxious, fearing they will make the wrong move and face punishment or negative consequences.

Authoritative parents don't actually rule. They demonstrate with love and compassionate caring. The child of an authoritative parent never doubts he is loved. He/she knows he/she can approach the parent without fear of ridicule or repercussion. There is always open dialogue.

The child grows up feeling secure that the parent will always support him/her.

By examining cohesive families that have grown up together, it is clear that most of the parents would be classified as authoritative. The children, even as grown adults, still love and respect their parents. Such families are intensely connected. That doesn't mean they never face problems or tragedies, but they deal with such negative setbacks with love, compassion, and understanding. They rely and lean on each other during difficult times. They function as one, having inherited their world. They demonstrate the daily dynamic equivalent of inheriting the earth through meekness. In short, authoritative parents guide their children humbly, and their family lives in a connected space that engenders lifelong love. The authoritarian parent rules arrogantly, fostering separation and alienation that can take a lifetime to work through.

Friendship

Think of the different types of friendship in which you are involved. As a prime example of adult friendships, let's consider the people you work with, those with whom you share common professional experiences, common relationships with authority figures, common compensation arrangements, and common challenges in progressing through the professional ranks. I will use my own life experiences to illustrate various friendships that can form in the workplace.

Medical education residency programs are where medical school graduates work in a practice setting, typically a hospital. This is typically a number of similarly aged young people who recently graduated from medical school, brought together bound by the desire to be trained to practice in their chosen specialty. The range in relationships between those involved in such programs, runs from best friends for life to mortal enemies.

I recently gave a eulogy for a man I met when I was chief resident, and he was one of my incoming interns, a first-year resident, with whom I made an immediate connection. We remained best friends for life, acting as best man for each other, weathering divorces, newborns, the struggles of our children, illness, major career choices, and milestones in life.

There were others with whom I never connected. We lacked respect for each other professionally, and we faced fundamentally different values as human beings. As we went off into our separate practices, we were barely cordially supportive of each other's career choices. If one of these should ever call, because he needed me for something, I would like to think I would respond, because I'd do that for anyone in need. However, we would never be considered friends.

What is the difference? What makes two people connect as friends, while others are never able to make such a connection and become distant for life?

This is another example of humility vs. arrogance.

Consider the arguments you have with those close to you. This usually happens when your sense of self is threatened, and you become fearful. That's the arrogant position, and it doesn't represent your true self. Deepak Chopra talks of connecting with true consciousness, the essence of who you really are, from which comes love, compassion, creativity, and a true sense of doing what's best for all. That is the connection, springing from humility. It is meekness. When you live from that place, you discover your joy, not the constant conflict living arrogantly provides, with its constant need to defend yourself.

Watch a group of preschoolers. They connect naturally. They humbly assume there are no significant differences among them. That's their default position. They like the same toys, and, before their humility is corrupted by adult-motivated arrogance and separation, they share everything, including snacks, games, other friends, and family members.

Before they learn to distrust and fear others who are different, they don't see the differences, much less fear other kids. They're connected, all part of the same inherited earth.

If you bring a preschooler into a gathering of people of all ages, genders, body sizes, and skin colors, and, if the preschooler hasn't been affected by his parents' fears and prejudices, he will connect with everyone. They are humble and almost completely lack the ability to stay within themselves.

Then there are the children who have been—and I use this word carefully—corrupted by adult arrogance. Those children are cautious and unwilling to speak to someone taller.

The humble, nonfearful kids are able to connect. They can see through the crowd to find those who are like them—other kids. They seek each other out, find each other, and connect. Then they play together, share toys, and, before long, are laughing, hugging, and holding hands, because they want to bring the other home with them.

Some might argue that this phenomenon proves the alternative view. Detractors to the BATM approach will say that people can't naturally connect with those who aren't like themselves. It's basic human nature arrogantly to see ourselves as separate from each other. It's natural to be fearful and apprehensive with anyone who isn't like us.

Children, especially young children, trust in those like themselves who haven't yet been corrupted by adult arrogance, fear, and separation. They may be naïve to fear and hatred, but they're also smart. To be safe, they connect with those they know they can trust, who will trust them in return.

In my book, *Moondance to Eternity,* I made the point that children possess an ingrained faith, the unshakable knowledge that, even at the time of death, they'll be all right. Their faith is so strong that often, just before death, they try to comfort their parents, then they ask their parents for permission to let their bodies pass away. It's an incredible phenomenon to witness, one that is very beautiful, and I have seen it many times. Those experiences formed the core of *Moondance to Eternity*.

The faith those children possess that all will be well, even after death, is similar to their intrinsic trust in other human beings, especially before they have been indoctrinated into the "stranger danger" mentality. The corruption of this faith is a metaphor to our human tendency to become fearful of those who are different.

We must learn from this. Many parents will argue, especially in these difficult times characterized by human trafficking and school shootings, that kids need to be cautious of strangers for their own safety. While that is true as a reflection of certain problems in society today, it is also true there is no question that the ability for children and all humans to connect with each other is impeded by the fear that comes from arrogance and separation.

How does this understanding translate into human relationships going forward? The lesson is that we must acknowledge the fact that we must always keep ourselves safe. There are some individuals in the world, such as sociopaths, liars, and con artists, from whom we must keep our distance for our own safety and survival. That reality aside, however, we can also learn from children and those who haven't yet learned to fear others who are different. If we humbly and meekly accept the fact that all human beings are fundamentally alike, we need not fear them, and thus we can connect with them.

Thus far I have offered a series of fundamental human relationships in an attempt to identify how we can utilize humility rather than arrogance to improve the connection between human beings in those relationships. The next part of this book will examine fundamental human values, those which are somehow integral to how we relate to one another, and examine them through the lens of humility over arrogance. My goal is to help others look at their own relationships and the personal values and characteristics that affect them. Successful relationships are key to fulfilling, successful lives, something most of us have as a goal in living our lives.

PART THREE

HUMAN VALUES FROM A HUMBLE POINT OF VIEW

CHAPTER 3

Love

Love is the most-talked-about, researched, understood, and yet misunderstood human emotional experience. It is most written about in books, plays, song lyrics, and TV shows, yet most of us struggle to find it and work incredibly hard to keep it once we do. There is either a humble or arrogant approach to love. As with everything else discussed in this book, the humble approach is outside oneself and is truly connected. The arrogant approach to love is self-centered and egocentric.

One of my favorite movies is *Dan in Real Life.* Steve Carrell. plays a widower trying to raise three vibrant daughters. After standing in the way of his middle daughter's romance with a boy, she angrily says he doesn't understand her, life, or love. She calls him a "murderer of love," then states, "Love isn't an emotion. It's an ability!"

That's an interesting concept that unpacks some truth. True love takes work and is often associated with the kind of pain that accompanies hard work.

Why does it take work? Because in its truest, humblest form, it's selfless. It requires the individual who is doing the loving to deny himself. Ironically, in denying oneself and giving love to another person in its most-powerful form, one must be honest with oneself about his own true nature.

I'm on my third and final marriage. Although I finally found the perfect partner for who I am, someone with whom I'm willing to live a life of sacrifice that brings true joy, I first had to find myself. That was a very difficult, sixty-year process.

My first marriage occurred when I was far too young. In my early twenties and in medical school, I was still an emotional child and had no idea what motivated people. I believed what I saw on TV and in the movies, that falling in love meant meeting someone who made me feel tingly at first. After getting to know that person, I would realize we had a lot in common, including interests and goals. I thought it would be as easy as the movies and sitcoms showed. If it felt good, it must be right.

I was not yet a fully formed adult human being, and I was sadly mistaken. I didn't know myself, which meant I wasn't in a position to give the love my wife needed to feel fulfilled. One might argue she wasn't ready to love, either, and that was also true.

To effectively love another human being, one must love himself first. That sounds counterintuitive. If love is supposed to be selfless, how would it not be selfish to love oneself?

It's selfless, because it first requires knowing yourself completely. Because we're all human, we have flaws, imperfections, shame, and humiliation. To love yourself requires accepting all your flaws and loving yourself anyway. That requires humility, which leads to connection.

If someone is humble about himself, knowing his own weaknesses, dreams, and expectations, then accepting more easily means accepting oneself and connecting with yourself. Without connecting or loving oneself, a person won't be able to love another. Further, without knowing oneself, it's impossible to accept and love others.

That all might seem obvious, and the expression might even be considered hackneyed and trite, but it raises questions. How does loving oneself equate with humility and connection? At its extreme, doesn't it seem narcissistic? While dwelling on oneself, it seems like it should produce a disconnection due to insincerity and unauthenticity.

Using the lens of humility vs. arrogance, how might one approach the problem of loving oneself in order to be emotionally available to others? The key is honesty. Living yourself requires brutal honesty about who you really are, with your foibles, faults, inadequacies, and sins.

Here's the humble part—to love yourself, you need to accept all your characteristics, all your past, all your sins, and forgive yourself for them. You must realize you are human and move on. Further, when you try to connect with another person, perhaps love that person, you can't fake who you are or misrepresent yourself in any way. You must accept, love, and appreciate your characteristics. Only then will you be able humbly to love another and give the relationship what it needs to succeed.

The arrogant approach separates. Although arrogance might achieve success in fostering early, superficial relationships, in the long term they won't endure, because they lack authenticity. Those who approach others with arrogance, including those they purport to love, do so from a position of "other." In a family context, they seek to foster the *appearance* of love, harmony, and mutual respect.

The extreme of this is the abusive relationship, often carried out by a narcissist who sees everything as a reflection of himself and how he appears. That isn't humble, because there is no connection, no acknowledgement of the fundamental "sameness" of other human beings. The abuser makes the relationship appear as if it's authentic by asserting power over the family members. They appear attached to the abuser, often a father or husband, because they fear reprisals against them if they don't act like they have a normal relationship.

For the narcissistic abuser, the ultimate arrogant non-attacher, it isn't about love, just loyalty. In exchange for the appearance of love, the abuser spouse or parents requires complete loyalty.

I heard during the impeachment hearings for President Trump that those who require constant attention (narcissists), also thirst for complete power (authoritarianism). A kind, compassionate, giving parent or romantic partner loves by caring more about the family members' or partner's experiences or emotions more than their own. Arrogant, self-centered love does the opposite.

What is the advantage of being a meek, humble lover of others? As the beatitude says, the meek shall inherit. I have already illustrated how the humble person who more successfully connects with others will inherit the earth.

Jon Donne wrote centuries ago, *No man is an island*. He knew what the writers of the beatitudes knew even earlier. We weren't put on earth to survive alone, separated from others. We were meant to connect, to care for each other, and to form relationships. Indeed, we were placed on this earth in these human bodies, which transport our souls through eternity, to form connections and bond with other people sharing similar experiences. We are better, stronger, more compassionate, and more loving when we connect. Remaining separate from each other out of arrogance assures our mutual destruction and misery.

Empathy/Compassion

This issue, the arrogant lack of the ability to feel the pain of others, is the crux of the power of humility over arrogance. In the midst of the House of Representatives Judiciary Committee hearings on the impeachment of President Trump, Representative Gomert said, "This reminds me of the trial of Socrates, where 501 jurors convicted him of arrogance. It seems like we are putting the president on trial for arrogance. You would find a lot of Republicans who would agree that he is arrogant. He has a lot to be arrogant about, but arrogance isn't a crime of misdemeanor."

What I took from that statement were the words, "He has a lot to be arrogant about." Was the speaker promoting, revering, and admiring arrogance? If so, then my book becomes even more important than I thought. If we choose arrogance over humility, we lose what has always been one of the best features of our culture and country—caring for others.

The beatitude encourages and admonishes us to embrace humility or meekness, as the way to connect with each other. My point is that such a connection always makes us stronger, more successful, and more compassionate toward each other.

As discussed in the section on Love, it's the humble, empathic approach to those with whom we have relationships that lead to ultimate success and optimizes the joy we can achieve in life.

Just before Thanksgiving each year, my family and I volunteer at a wonderful institution in Tampa called the Metropolitan Ministries. They offer a holiday meal opportunity for low-income and other deserving folk who might not be able to afford the usual part of an American Thanksgiving. According to the size of their families, the people go shopping down aisles of donated foods, hoping to obtain enough for the holiday, including turkey or ham for their families.

Each year, we bring our teenagers and a few friends to this venue, where we each grab shopping carts and wait in line to escort a designated family member through the aisles, helping them achieve their hopes for a well-rounded meal.

To do this successfully, we must be able to engage and connect with the shoppers, which requires empathy, a degree of compassion, and humility. Arrogance stands in the way of connecting with these folks and providing them with a meal.

At one point during the most-recent Thanksgiving shopping experience, I watched my incredible wife escort a thirty-something woman alone down the grocery aisles. My stepdaughter and I were escorting another woman, helping her choose food items for her family, when my wife suddenly caught my eye.

"John," she called, "I want you to meet April (not her real name). She has seven foster kids at home, and she's shopping for all of them!"

Having seen countless foster families and kids in my pediatric practice, then assisting my wife as a volunteer in the Guardian ad Litem program, I always felt such people were heroes, the epitome of altruism and compassion. They had to be very humbly connected with those in need and struggling, be they kids in need (often victims of abuse or neglect) or those with complex medical problems unable to be handled by their birth families.

I applauded the young woman and shouted, "Bravo!" She beamed with pride.

There are so many demonstrations of empathy and compassion in that little slice of our lives. Not only did I see it in the wonderful family members, who often had to swallow their pride to provide minimal holiday food for their families. I also saw it in the kids who volunteered to help these folks shop.

When we returned to the car at the end of the event, after the teens' mandatory whining that the activity took up so much of their day, I caught a feeling of joyfulness and giddiness from them. That was the joy that comes from connection, which can only result from humility. By connecting with those in the community who were less fortunate, we connected with each other. By connecting with the better angels of our natures, the humble forces that allowed us to connect and help, we also connected better with ourselves.

That was the image of our family inheriting the earth, as the beatitude said, and I hoped it was an activity we could continue each Thanksgiving as long as we were physically able. By connecting with others and helping those in need by humbly taking on such a responsibility, we opened our souls to connection, joy, and love in its truest, most-profound sense. In the car driving home, we had laughter, singing, and joy—all manifestations of that love.

In my 1968 book, I introduced the concepts of *Integrity* and the *Trinity Operating System* (to know and then love oneself). In the current book, what started as a reflection on the most-tumultuous year in modern history turned into a metaphor for my own spiritual journey, characterized mainly by hiding from my true feelings on controversial subjects to avoid rejection. It evolved into a primer about knowing oneself, being true to one's inner nature, and making decisions based on being honest.

I coined the concept of one's sense of self having three realms, the intrinsic self (the most-honest, truest core values one has, analogous to Freud's id); the extrinsic self (the self others see, like Freud's ego); and the observational self (what you see when you observe yourself interacting with others, Freud's superego). When one's self is identical in all three spheres, which is what we strive for once we can be emotionally honest about what we feel, we achieve integrity. Once we attain that, we are more able humbly and honestly to interact with the world in a more-fulfilling, rewarding manner.

Connection and attachment are more successful when one has humbly done the work to know oneself, accept it, and share. We achieve integrity by having our intrinsic, extrinsic, and observational selves in line. Humility comes in with the acceptance of the reality of our real self. That gets complicated. It might be OK to choose to be the best person you can be, but it's unhealthy to try to become someone completely opposite of your actual character. Although it sounds a bit abstract, it's important.

I was trapped in a thirty-year marriage with my second wife, with the biggest problem being I was afraid to be myself. I acted, thought, and expressed myself in ways I felt were expected. Why? Because I was afraid. Afraid of what? Mostly I feared rejection. If I wasn't the person my wife at the time expected me to be, I would be rejected and unloved.

The problem is, one can follow that paradigm only so long before one loses one's sense of self completely. Without a sense of self, we can't form attachments. The irony is, in trying not to be rejected by a partner, a humble connection can't occur, and one can easily wind up living alone, feeling profoundly lonely and desperate. Such desperation results in acting out, which can destroy a marriage.

I later found a relationship based completely on honesty, of being myself, and it resulted in a profound, lifelong attachment. It took me awhile, but I finally figured it out.

Faith/Spirituality

Spirituality is defined as the understanding that we are all connected as humans, and that the spirit of that connection is guided by a force greater than ourselves. In traditional Christianity, that connection is referred to as compassion, and the force greater than ourselves is God.

The understanding that we are basically the same and connected is a humble philosophy. The arrogant approach to spirituality is exclusive, because anyone different is excluded from the group. Truly spiritual groups, including organized religions, are inclusive. They accept all regardless of apparent differences by recognizing that their souls are connected. The others are driven by the same human needs, and the organizing force to their lives, individually and as a group, is a force greater than themselves.

Faith also requires acceptance. For acceptance, humility is absolutely essential. In *Moondance to Eternity*, I detailed some of my experiences with chronically ill children, many of whom eventually died. I chronicled many situations in which the children demonstrated a feeling of peace and resolve even at their deaths. I learned children have an intrinsic sense of trust. They humbly accept and seem to have innate knowledge of what every organized religion tries to teach—that even in death, they will be OK. The parents always struggled more than the kids, often out of arrogance. They felt their child was dying because of something we adults should have been able to control. Either someone made a mistake, something was overlooked, or a disease wasn't properly prevented. What we learn from the humility of sick children is that we don't always have an explanation for or any control over human frailty, especially illness.

Parents often argue they simply don't want to lose their children, and that's why they react to critical illness as if it was a loss of control. After all, parents spend much of their kids' childhood trying to prevent negative things from happening, especially illness and death. Children, however, humbly accept that we have no control over the randomness of disease, trauma, or death, and thus they accept and often have to teach us to be peaceful in acceptance.

That is, very simply, an example of faith. Kids seem to have it naturally. Like hatred, they must learn to have no faith. They learn from friends, family members, media, and many other sources. They are seduced to learn by arrogance, the need to separate out of fear. Arrogance drives away their humility. Consequently, they lose their faith. They are easily convinced, as are we all, that our experience is unique to the world, different from anything anyone else could have felt.

Those who keep their faith throughout the vicissitudes of life remain humble. They keep their spirituality sound, recognizing that we are, as humans, all connected, guided by a force greater than ourselves.

In my church, we decided to take the new year, starting with the current decade, by reading the Bible one section per day, hoping to complete it by the end of 2020. Our pastor presented a new slant on Genesis, which to me pointed out the reward of humility and the risk of arrogance, as well as God's power of forgiveness.

The pastor said that Adam and Eve ate the apple in the Garden of Eden not so much out of disobedience as out of arrogance. The serpent told them the truth—eating from the Tree of Knowledge would give them the same understanding as God about the ways of the world, particularly the nature of good and evil.

Would we be better off as a race if we hadn't gained that understanding so early in our history? I doubt it matters. The issue can be debated for centuries to come. Perhaps the story was meant to tell us that, because of our free will, we would ultimately be ruled by the curiosity to find out the knowledge from the tree and live with the consequences.

Since we ate the apple, God said, "OK, now you've done it. You can't be Me, but you can understand some of the issues we will face on earth, perhaps a little better than you would have otherwise. You'll be better off if you humbly accept the fact that you are all humans and will face the struggle between free will and My hopes for you for eternity. Some of it will hurt. You will screw up, but I'll always be there for you and will protect you by providing you with choices you can make."

Throughout most of the rest of the Old Testament, humility is rewarded, and arrogance, which is defined as men trying to be God, is punishable by the consequences of unfortunate, arrogant decisions. In the new Testament, Jesus reiterates that by telling us in the Sermon on the Mount in 5 Matthew, "Blessed are the meek, for they shall inherit the earth."

Fundamentalism, which has been increasing for the last fifty years, is arrogance in the extreme. It may have begun with the Islamic revolution in Iran in the 1970s, the taking of American hostages, and the revolutionary fundamentalism headed by the Ayatollah Khomeini. Even the sectarian violence between Shia and Sunni Muslims is fueled by the arrogance that one's beliefs are righter and more accurate than another's.

We see the same thing in Christian fundamentalism. It seems like normal tribalism, almost a corrupt form of team spirit. If done humbly, it wouldn't be so damaging. It's human nature to want to think that one's club, team, or religion is the best, but when fueled by the arrogance that one faith is better or righter than another, it becomes horribly destructive, fueling wars, hatred, and death. Even within denominations, there are struggles fueled by the disconnection borne out of arrogance, with conservatives vs. liberals and traditionalists vs. progressives.

In the Netflix movie, *The Two Popes,* about conversations between the last two popes (Benedict while he was pope and Cardinal Bergoglio before he became Pope Frances), the two men were fundamentally different and disagreed on many things. Still, they spoke, shared wine and music, talked, and listened.

At the beginning of their conversations, they were arrogantly separated by their differences and their stubborn resolve to hold to their positions. They were both old men who had long lives, filled with regrets, mistakes, and memories of when they were called to the priesthood. Once they essentially confess to one another, they demonstrate humility and manage a deep connection. At some level, they became friends. Humility connected them after their arrogance disconnected them.

Pope Benedict, after first being appalled by some of the lifestyle choices and philosophies of the future pope, once he connected with him and accepted him as a fellow cleric and human being, finally realizes that for the future of the church, he should retire and leave an opening for Frances to become pope, because that was best for the world.

At a crucial moment in the film, after Benedict eats dinner alone, leaving Frances alone to eat his, they meet in a very regal sitting room to relax. Frances again mentions he would like to retire as a cardinal, but that requires the Pope's permission, which was his reason for his trip to Rome. Each time he mentioned the idea, Benedict countered him, and their exchanges became increasingly contentious.

When Brogolio brought it up again, in that after-dinner meeting, Benedict said, "Not now. Let us just be together, quietly, enjoying each other's company."

To me, that was the moment when they connected. It was followed by scenes where they became more intimate friends, discussing their pasts and truths they learned. While they were just being together, they humbly and silently accepted each other, no longer arrogantly trying to best the other person. One could argue, that these were the actions of men who affected the lives of billions of people, their ability to be humble, or their meekness, allowed them to inherit the earth. Frances ultimately inherited Benedict's job, which would not have been possible without the two proud men facing each other humbly.

While on the subject of Roman Catholicism, the religion in which I was raised and still feel an affinity for, despite my family's current Protestant practices, I want to discuss the Eucharistic liturgy—the communion practices. The Catholic Church stand strongly behind the position that only baptized Catholics may receive communion during Mass. To me, that's an exclusive approach, because it excludes people unless they meet the church's criteria for acceptance. It means the Catholic Church is a very exclusive club. It doesn't accept or connect, because it rejects and disconnects many.

I have met priests who approach communion in their masses as accepting. One in particular once said that the decision to take communion during Mass was between the individual and his God. It didn't need to be dictated by archaic rules. Such a progressive attitude would be seen as heresy by many traditionalists, like many in my family of earlier generations.

Probably in an effort to recruit new members by demonstrating their inclusiveness over Catholic exclusive, our United Methodist Church invites all who want it to receive communion. They don't have to be members of our church or of any church. They simply must want to receive the sacrament and do it prayerfully. That humility is connecting, and, I believe, more in keeping with the intention of the early church. Jesus Himself sought to accept all into His church.

Health/Medicine

We live in a period of unprecedented interest in personal health, wellness, and disease treatment and prevention. There are several ways that the humility/arrogance duality can enter into the way one approaches personal health and fitness. Arrogance takes root in several respects, preventing people from achieving optimal health. One is the manner in which we view our own health.

As a physician, our tendency is often to think that somehow, we are immune from the illness we see in patients. That's magical thinking, though. It's as if we feel we have power over the diseases we treat in others.

I have a difficult genetic makeup when it concerns heart disease and cancer. One or both of those will strike at some time in my life. In 2011, when I was in the late stages of an earlier marriage and had reached a particularly painful juncture, the anger and personal attacks reached a peak, and I started experiencing chest pain.

I knew I had borderline high blood pressure. Each time it was checked over the years, it was always high. I never addressed it with my doctors. I thought I had an acceptable lifestyle. It was true I was also overweight, and my eating habits needed changing. I liked to drink, although not excessively. I jogged three miles a day. I pooh-poohed my high blood pressure, claiming I had white-coat hypertension, or I was feeling stressed when it was taken.

That was arrogance. I had actual essential hypertension, but I remained in denial, because I feared becoming sick. I ignored it and arrogantly thought that if I didn't face it, it would magically vanish.

Instead, the damage grew over decades. Plaque built up in my coronary arteries, eventually leading to coronary artery disease, ischemia, angina, and, eventually, open-heart surgery. My recovery from surgery was dramatically delayed by a stroke, which affected functions on my left side, as well as swallowing, speech, and probably contributed to the profound depression I suffered after surgery.

What was intended to be a five-day hospital stay ended up lasting ten days in the cardiac intensive-care unit, a prolonged recovery, and the eventual realization that if I didn't face the reality of my metabolic syndrome and its risk to my life, I would be dead within months.

I was forced into humility. The resulting meekness connected me to the reality of myself and my vulnerabilities. It made me a more-honest human being, which aided my connection to others. Authenticity, vulnerability, and humility connect people.

There is also the arrogance of people who pay attention to their bodies, something I see in younger, healthy, even athletic people. They seem to believe that, if they do everything they read that is called "healthy," and always do the right thing, they will avoid illness and put off death. They don't understand how illness and death sometimes come to people who do everything right.

How do we humbly approach our own health? This is a "thread the needle" proposition.

We must start by humbly accepting the fact that our bodies are incredibly complex, finely tuned, poetically beautiful organisms with internal checks and balances. If the conditions are right, they trend inexorably toward health and healing.

Consider the immune system and its inflammatory response. When there is an injury, wound, or infection, the immune system is triggered to battle it and keep our amazing bodies healthy. Think about how quickly our bodies heal after an injury. In the case of a cut or laceration, the incredibly complex clotting cascade begins immediately. The wound stops bleeding and begins to heal, forming a fibrin clot, scab, and, eventually, a scar. I used to tell the nurses in the hospital who cared for critically ill children, "The body wants to heal and will do so unless we interrupt it or don't allow it. The point of medicine becomes to create an environment where healing can occur. If it's an infection, we provide antibiotics to kill the bacteria, so the body can proceed with healing itself through the immune system. If it's a wound, we close it to help it heal more effectively and more cleanly."

There's a delicate balance, similar to that between injury and healing, between arrogance and humility with one has to face personal health challenges. Arrogance comes into play when someone feels invulnerable to injury and illness because of eating healthy and staying in shape, having strong genes, or through the arrogance physicians sometimes feel, because they understand the pathology of a major illness, which makes them immune to it themselves.

Humility comes when people realize that no matter how healthy they are, there's no guarantee against accident or illness. Assuming someone wants to heal, if a person falls ill, he or she must give up control to the medical establishment, overcoming any fears, preconceived notions, or medical ignorance. Humility dictates that an ill person must come to grips with the fact that treatment might fail, and death might occur. In that case, humility requires strength and courage. The arrogant approach is actually that of a coward, mainly inspired by fear of acceptance.

In our own health care, how does arrogance separate and humility connect? One could argue that when one humbly confronts personal health or illness, one becomes more connected to oneself and is able to understand better the body and its subtleties more thoroughly. When you approach the body arrogantly, thinking one has power over one's health because you take good care of yourself, you fail to acknowledge that even someone in the best physical condition can become ill, have a car accident, or, God forbid, be involved in a random shooting event. This means the person is disconnected from the reality of his own health and his body.

If you approach your health humbly, saying, "I do what I can to preserve my health. I eat reasonably well, exercise, and try not to drink too much. I don't smoke, either. I need to realize, however, that life is vulnerable. There is an inevitable end to my earthly life, so I need a spiritual approach to life that transcends physical well-being."

Having such an attitude will not only connect someone to his body its relative wellness more closely. It also connects to a personal sense of

God and the universe, which connects him to the other inhabitants of that universe—his fellow human beings.

Arrogance in the Healthcare Industry

After practicing medicine in a hospital setting for thirty-five years, I've seen many examples of arrogance and humility in the practice of traditional Western medicine.

On the arrogant side are hospital administrators, insurance companies, big pharmacy, and caregivers with huge egos. What do they have in common? Their arrogance dictates that they are the reason for the healthcare around them, whether it comes through profit, megalomania, needy egos, or disdain for the sick. They are separated from those whom they care for, when the fact is that they are simply feeding their own egos, increasing their personal fortunes, or creating more control over the system.

Humility occurs in situations where the caregiver emphasizes with those being cared for, typically on the front lines of healthcare. One can see such humility at work in the inner city and rural clinics throughout America, where caregivers are typically part of the community they serve and are connected with their patients. For the humble, such a connection is so strong, their egos are fed only when the patient's suffering has been decreased.

One can see that in the healthcare policies many people argue about, which try to provide the most care to the largest number of people. As of this writing, hospitals are designed for, and insurance companies reimburse for, acute illness, severe trauma, and complex surgery. Preventative medicine, wellness, and health preservation are relegated to individuals or wellness centers and med spas, which offer people what they really want and need from healthcare providers. People want to look and feel their best.

Acute-care medicine is necessary, because people do become sick, accidents happen, and sometimes, surgery is needed. However, medicine connects most with people in preventative environments, where conversations and connections take place, where the caregiver comes to know the patient, understands his or her needs, and works hard to make true wellness happen within the context of the patients' unique lives.

In a recent *Time* article, the point was made that there may be too much surgery and too many expensive procedures and tests. These are motivated by giving patients the impression that everything is being done, there are possible concerns about malpractice suits, and there is general ignorance over nonsurgical solutions to complex problems. The humblest approach to heart disease could be to say, "Don't just do something, stand there!"

I must admit that, in the final years of my career in critical care, I didn't embrace such a concept. Out of fear, arrogance, and a desire to prove to everyone involved I was doing everything I could, I over treated. I will admit that I may have caused more problems and possibly harmed sick children by over treating, over consulting specialists, over testing, and overmedicating. Even when I was outdoing it, the medical community embraced me as one of the best, because I showed allegiance to the medical care system rather than the patients and their families. I sought redemption by changing my focus from acute care, where I lived in a conspiracy with a flawed healthcare model, to prevention and wellness, where the emphasis on patient care is education, inspiration, and motivation. The latter, I believe, is the humbler approach.

Insurance companies have not yet fully embraced the concept of reimbursing patients for preventative care. To receive help in their healthcare, patients must already be sick, which means having a pre-existing condition, further widening the gap between the sick and the well, the caregivers and those who require care. The current system is arrogant and cruel. In the future, if we wish truly to promote the health of individuals and society in general, the system must embrace a humbler, kinder organization and structure.

At the Bedside of Sick Kids

My book *Moondance to Eternity* was inspired by my experiences with sick and dying children. Nowhere else does the power of humility show itself. In medical training, we treat death as the enemy. As such, we fear it desperately. That is so true, that when physicians know someone is dying in a nearby room, we avoid it and leave the task of comforting the individual and the family to nursing and support staff.

I was one of those physicians who hid from death and ran from its victims, until one day, I met a special patient. His name was Alex, and I wrote about him in *Moondance*. He faced death fearlessly, holding to the faith that once he died and even in death, "Everything will be all right."

I learned to do the same. After Alex, I no longer shied away from dying children. I learned that being involved with those emotional, intimate family moments is a privilege and is, perhaps, one of the best parts of being a critical-care physician. The moment of death, misunderstood and feared by most people, is actually a beautiful passage to the next phase, which none of us understand, but faith asks us to accept humbly with courage and comfort.

My humble connections came with accepting my own similarity to the dying patients for whom I cared, accepting I was no different from them. I was not immune. I couldn't stave off death no matter what I did. Why not accept death as part of life and stop fearing it? Humbly accepting death connects us to the most-human experience of all, and it brings us closer to all of humanity. What better way to inherit the earth?

Humility brings connection. When I had the humility to tell a family honestly, "We have done all we can do for your child medically. While miracles do happen, we have to be honest with you and tell you that your child is likely going to die tonight. We will do everything we can to make him as comfortable as possible. We will b e here with you when he passes. We know this is very hard, but it will be peaceful, and your child will command all our respect until the inevitable end comes."

Once that conversation took place, I experienced an unearthly peace at the patient's bedside. Intense connections formed between the family and caregiver. All present in the room were strongly connected with the dying child.

Unfortunately, many if not most ICU caregivers are more arrogant. They find themselves separated from the child and family. They are unable to connect with death or the dying child, because in the arena of death, the caregivers are filled with fear and misunderstanding.

CHAPTER 4

Money—Problem or Solution?

I never took an economics class, although I wish I had. I make out quarterly payroll for my small corporation. I haven't done my own taxes in decades. That's why God gave us accountants. I can't use an Excel spreadsheet, nor can I write a profit-and-loss report.

I've had plenty of life experience, though, both making lots of money and losing almost as much. Please note that I wrote *losing,* not *spending.* I'm not lamenting losing money. Through humility, I learned more about the world, human nature, and even myself during the times I lost money than when I was financially successful. I daresay I became a better man after losing a fortune than making one. The other important lesson I learned was that much of the winning/losing dichotomy was out of my control.

I don't advocate Communism, mainly because even its economic model is almost always corrupted by opportunistic dictators who enrich themselves at the expense of the general population, even though they claim to be representing the good of the whole over the needs of the individual. Somehow, they don't seem to consider themselves one of those individuals who must sacrifice for the greater good. That is a phenomenon where humility is corrupted by arrogance.

It's a troubling paradox about the capitalistic model that when someone succeeds and becomes wealthy, someone else has to fail and become impoverished. Humility could be used as an antidote by the fortunate wealthy to connect with those who haven't succeeded as well, generously assisting the less fortunate.

That practice, however, is difficult to put into action. Greed has a malignant, infectious character. Once humans are touched by material success, they want more and forget about those less fortunate. The arrogance of that mentality is obvious and proves how, in real life, the struggle of humility over arrogance can be extremely challenging.

Although I believe empathy and humility are our human default settings, arrogance, once learned, is exceedingly difficult to unlearn. It gives itself the appearance of being a true part of human nature. Some may remember Gordon Ghecko saying in *Wall Street*, "Greed is good," touting greed as an essential American value. Once someone accumulates significant wealth, often by beating someone else out of those funds, greed and arrogance become addictive and almost impossible to stop.

My children all asked me at different points over the years which profession would assure them a comfortable living. Actually, they asked how to become rich while working the least. I constantly told them, perhaps idealistically, that it didn't matter what they did as long as they did their absolute best and loved what they did. If they were lucky enough to find a profession that met those requirements, the money would take care of itself.

I still believe that is true, but, in thinking about this book, I realized that it involves the humility to give up control, or "giving it up to God," as some might say. Arrogance, however, claims it has complete control over everything.

Making money and being successful requires others to appreciate and want to reward someone. One thing no one can control is how others react to them or what others' opinions of them might be. The ultimate act of humility is to tell yourself that you are a mere human who has no control over anything except your own behavior. All you can do is your best and let the rest take care of itself.

Arrogant people feel they deserve to be rewarded in a certain way for how hard they worked or all the hoops they jumped through to get where they are. The universe has so many variables, however—God works in mysterious ways, right?—that we can't plan on too much. It's unrealistic and arrogant if we try. Illness alone, which by definition is unpredictable, renders any planning an exercise in futility.

I digressed from the theme of this section, money and economy, but I hope I illustrated the connection. My advice to young people who ask how they can make a comfortable living is to do what they can to optimize their situation through education, attitude, and responsible work and study habits. However, that alone won't guarantee a positive outcome, wealth, or security. The humble way is, after doing your best over the things you can control, to relax and gratefully take whatever happens as a gift that allows you to grow, learn, be reassured, or forced to change. Through gratitude, one can find contentment that overcomes any disappointment.

Gratitude—the Humble Approach

To be truly grateful, we need to appreciate all our experiences are gifts, even those that are disappointments.

During the summer of 2015, I was in a very dark place. I was recovering from open-heart surgery, struggling to control the risk factors that contributed to my heart disease. I had been divorced for a year at that time and felt intensely lonely while struggling to reconnect with my adult children who sided with my ex-wife in our contentious divorce. I had just moved into an apartment after realizing I couldn't afford to live in the house where I'd been. I worked part-time for a weight-loss company and felt unsatisfied and uncertain about what the future held for me personally or professionally.

One Sunday afternoon, I dozed in front of the TV, putting off a trip to the grocery store across the street from my apartment building. When I finally decided to get up off my aging butt and go, I grabbed my sustainable shopping bag, splashed water on my face, and emerged from my bachelor pad to begin my journey across the street to the grocery store.

When I arrived at the bank of elevators to begin my descent to the sidewalk below, a pleasant, unassuming, quiet woman, somewhat younger than I, stood there, waiting for an elevator. We exchanged pleasantries and started conversing. We immediately connected, talking through our elevator trip and still talking while walking out onto the sidewalk, while crossing the street, going into the grocery store, and for forty-five minutes while in the market.

I never met her before despite the fact that we worked in similar fields and had friends and acquaintances in common. We exchanged numbers and agreed to stay in touch, but, because I felt cautious and a bit frightened by the power of our coincidental meeting, we didn't reconnect for several weeks.

When we did, we fell in love and hardly spent a day apart in the next five years. Last year, we married, with my new children acting as the wedding party.

Most people wouldn't consider a low point in life as a gift, but had I not been in such a dark place when I decided to go to the store that Sunday, I would never have met the woman who saved my life, gave me purpose, and renewed my strength and vitality.

I remain humbled by the miracles of misfortune that life presents. I suggest everyone should be open to re-examining the things in life that don't seem to be working. Face them with humility, accept them, connect with them, and be thankful they found you.

We also need to forgive ourselves for our pasts. That takes humility and the ability to embrace one's past, which makes us more empathic and able to connect with others who also have pasts—that means everyone. While I'm in a lifelong happy marriage now, my prior experience was fraught with sadness, loneliness, and pain. To regret that experience minimizes the beauty of my present situation, which could have only happened as a result of my previous situations, no matter how negative they felt at the time. It's like the dictum, "Don't sweat the small stuff, and it's all small stuff."

One can also say, "Be thankful for the experiences that make you the person you are and give you the life you're grateful for."

It's true that all experiences make you who you are, and therefore they are all blessings. We should be thankful for all of them. This humility connects you with the arc of your life and with wider humanity through the empathy you gain from a circumspect view of life.

Citizenship

The polarization of our current political climate seems perilous for the future of America. Still, it's our responsibility to be good citizens and custodians of our country's heritage. How can we do that? There is the humble approach and the arrogant approach.

We began this journey discussing how, as the age of Trump comes to a close—which it will unless he declares himself president for life—where arrogance, division, fear, and hatred have been our guiding principles, we must decide that we need a new, different way to approach our responsibilities as Americans. I used the word *responsibilities* because I'm naïve enough to believe the humble vision of John F. Kennedy. Some would not consider him humble after he said in his inaugural address of 1961, "Ask not what your country can do for you, ask what you can do for your country."

With Trump being acquitted in his impeachment trial, and his demonstration of anger, vindictiveness, and desire to seek revenge afterward, I fear the country is at an important juncture. The great thing about America is that the people are still in charge. Our opinions matter, and I believe most of us face our responsibilities from a humble standpoint. We are interested in the welfare of others, not just in propelling our own futures and fearing those who are different from us.

If anyone doesn't think we're being governed by an attitude of fear and hatred, look at how quickly Trump fired witnesses in the House impeachment hearings. He talked about "crazy, socialist Democrats," who, if they won, would rob the citizens of everything they worked for and change all their cherished values. Interestingly, the opposite seems to be true. If arrogance wins another term, we stand to lose our country's nature to aid those in need and recognize we're all fundamentally the same and are connected by that sameness.

We need to embrace the values that brought us together—equality, compassion, a representative republic, and the value of each individual. That takes meekness, the humility to understand that we're connected by our similarities. In a later chapter, I will explore the 2020 election more in depth without recommending any particular candidate but by exploring the principles we must re-embrace while rejecting the arrogance and disconnection that has characterized the current administration and trickled down to average Americans.

We must remember the humility that surrounded the start of our nation. The founders were a group of revolutionary leaders, who may have been driven by ego, who came up with a new form of government where one individual didn't have more power than another, a system that was dependent on the will of the people.

Communication was key in the development of our early nation. The truth needed to be spread to many people. In that environment, rumors spread rapidly. Ironically, we now live in a world characterized by rapid, available forms of communication, where virtually everyone carries in a pocket the ability to communicate to the rest of the world and look at all the known facts accumulated by humanity so far, but we still sometimes believe a piece of misinformation found on the Internet over knowledge and facts we know are accurate.

Psychologists point to something called Motivational Thinking as the characteristic to explain that phenomenon. It states that we believe facts that follow a certain paradigm, an attitude and approach we already have.

In the time immediately following Trump's acquittal at the end of the impeachment trial, we saw examples of facts that were disputed or even agreed upon, but whose effects were disagreed upon. In some cases, different groups held entirely different facts.

We live in a complicated binary, dualistic, political culture, where one is almost required to see the world one way or the other. On one side, Trump extorted a foreign power to gather negative information on a possible election adversary, compromising national interest for his personal gain.

Another side saw the president's action as being tough and strong, something that needed to be done to promote his re-election, which they feel is definitely in the nation's best interests. In America at this time, if one believes a certain scenario, one must also believe Trump must be defeated at all costs.

Humility suggests we remain open enough to see another person's point of view. Perhaps that was what Christ meant when He said to love our enemies. It doesn't mean to attach oneself to those enemies or accept their mistreatment but to respect them enough to see their point of view. We live in an arrogant time, where conservatives watch Fox News and liberals watch MSNBC, seeing stories from outlets that support and largely agree with one's personal view.

That isn't what the framers of our country had in mind when they created the checks and balances of the three branches of government and the bicameral legislature. By definition, they must work together to accomplish goals.

In the present day, I believe it's our civic duty and in the interests of the connection that comes with humility to find common ground. If we could find the things we have in common, the issues that literally bind us, perhaps the acrimony that characterizes these times could subside. We could once again, like at other crucial moments in history when all were tested, come together in recognition of our common needs, acknowledge our common adversaries, and overcome them together.

Education—the Humility of Overcoming Ignorance

The educational process is wracked with the battle of arrogance vs. humility at all levels. Whether it's the battle between public and private education, the intrinsic biases in the academic hierarchy, the dynamic between educator and student, or the ongoing battle of prayer in schools, an arrogant approach separates parties and leads to acrimony. The humble approach leads to connection, unity, and a better outcome for all.

In his 2020 State-of-the-Union address, Trump referred to public schools as "government schools." The insinuation and reference to his followers was unmistakable. There are certain individuals, particularly those inhabiting the political right in America, who think that the public school system is a liberal establishment indoctrination tool to create followers for the left's agenda. That is arrogance, which leads to division over curriculum, over which private citizens have input through the school boards, and in the structure of the faculty and the individual hires within specific schools and school systems.

Where citizens, students, and adults humbly approach their educational institutions as allies where all are interesting in educating the young in the interest of improving the community and ensuring the future, that connection leads to progress and a warm sense of community. In small towns, suburbs, and urban villages, the school is often the center of the community, and teachers are among the community's most-valued members. Humility is at the core of such relationships. Students, parents, teachers, administrators, and taxpayers are connected as humble participants in a team effort to educate the young. The heart of these American institutional relationships is love and understanding.

I would like to drill down into the student/teacher relationship and the commitment to learning.

I once had an elementary teacher ask the class, "Why do you think I teach you?"

After the expected answers, like, "you want to make money," one wise guy who said, "You didn't go to college long enough to do anything else," or someone who said, "Because you like to yell at us," a thoughtful student raised his hand and said, "To teach us to teach ourselves."

The teacher stopped the class and said, "That's it!" He explained learning is a lifelong process. The purpose of schooling was to educate the student to be able to educate himself later in life. Such an idealistic approach, and the true purpose of organized education, however, soon is lost when arrogance and competition take over.

Competition requires arrogance, which separates students from making connections. I don't advocate that every student shouldn't try his best to learn as much as he can. I'm saying that competition tempered with humility can lead to a better connection and better life lessons for children who have been programmed by parents, teachers, and the education system to beat all the other students.

It has been suggested that we don't teach our children enough about the importance of kindness, caring, and compassion. The system trains them to be arrogant, and that makes it very difficult for them to connect with other students or learn how to connect with adults later in life.

When we're at the dinner table after school, rather than emphasizing grades, test scores, success, or failure, we might consider asking the kids, "Who did you help today?" or "Did you teach a slower student something today?" or "How did the class perform on the test day?" instead of "How did you do today?" Worse would be, "Did you do better than your friend, Erica, today?"

I see high school and college students who confuse academic performance with their relative worth as human beings. That's an arrogant approach that leads to comparison, excessive competition, and disconnection. Some schools have found they can better control the rampant epidemics of depression, drug abuse, sexual abuse, and suicide by fostering a sense of community where students are more supportive of each other's education and professional goals than they are competitive. The results, thus far, have been promising.

A common denominator of depression, suicide, and drug abuse is loneliness, separation, and disconnection. The traditional education system, with pressure for grades, intense competition, and dwindling education funding, doesn't support a sense of family, connection, or compassion. Perhaps a humbler approach would support connection and thereby dramatically improve the educational experience and contentment during higher education.

PART FOUR

The Humble Life: Trump, the Pandemic, and More

CHAPTER 5

The Evolving Family, the Case for Humility, and Connection

In a recent edition of the *Atlantic,* David Brooks published a thought-provoking article on the demise of the nuclear family. The nuclear family is the idea of a family unit made popular in the mid-20th century. Even today, it is considered the model for family structure for the last fifty years. However, the model has been changing over recent decades and continues to evolve in the 21st century.

Brooks made the point that, at the dawn of civilization, man gathered into groups, usually of 20-25 individuals, to care for each other, hunt, gather together, seek shelter, protect each other, and, eventually after the Neolithic revolution, to farm land together.

These groups weren't necessarily genetically related. Only in the latter half of the second millennium did people congregate in groups that were defined as family. In the years after World War Two, as evidenced by my own childhood, kinship groups consisted of grandparents, who were typically immigrants from other countries, their children, and their grandchildren. That was an exceedingly useful group, because the children were always surrounded by cousins, aunts, uncles, and grandparents. The generations knew each other, cared about each other, and, when someone in the family was sick or in trouble, the group rose to offer assistance.

By the turn of the 21st century, the nuclear family was dissolving. Younger generations moved to the suburbs to live in single-family homes, separated by expansive lawns, and spending time in their automobiles. When they were home, people sat in front of TV sets.

Where major holidays were once characterized by multigenerational family units around a large table, talking, laughing, and supporting each other, the current mode for families who gather for the holidays is to have smaller groups, often consisting of one set of parents and their children. They might possibly add some close friends or relatives. Often, the TV is on, giving people an excuse to watch a parade, a dog show, Thanksgiving football, or their favorite Christmas movie.

Brooks traced that sociological trend by saying that families once gathered around the holiday table, then they gathered around the TV, and then the individuals began staring at their personal screens without relating to anyone else.

However, there is hope. On the *Drs. John and Lisa Show*, Tuesdays at 12:10, live on Facebook, later posted on Facebook and YouTube, we have made the point many times that human beings are programmed for attachment. For optimal health, we need to be connected with others. To connect, we must humbly accept that we are fundamentally similar to other people. Through that sense of meekness, we can connect and inherit the earth.

During the height of the AIDS epidemic in the 1980s, particularly in places like San Francisco, Brooks points out that homosexual men and lesbian women, many of whom were rejected by their own families, formed kinship groups and communal living situations. They took care of each other, pooling their talents for the kinship group and the individuals within it.

Once again due to economic pressure, there are signs that people are rediscovering ways to reconnect with family and larger kinship groups. Kids in college form tight friendships that resemble families in many respects. They have closer relationships with their parents, upon whom they depend for financial support, than we did in my generation in the mid-20th century. More Millennials are moving back home with their parents, and more seniors are moving in with their children and other relatives.

I believe we'll find kinship groups within which we can live and work. The groups may be based on genetic family relationships or other economic or noneconomic needs. In any event, they will be based on the absolute fact that we aren't designed to go through life alone. For optimal health, we need to be attached to other humans.

During the coronavirus pandemic, the family experience has been turned on its head. Whatever family or kinship group we have, we're hunkered down in that group for the foreseeable future. True, though we work together, divide tasks, and try to keep each other healthy, our patience is often worn thin. With two teenagers home from school, and since I'm not as young as I once was, I find myself gaining the reputation of a grump. Still, it gave me time to write this book, so I shouldn't complain.

It is a test of true humility to realize we're all in this together and experience the same feelings of uncertainty, fear, helplessness, and tedium. When the kids drive me crazy, or when my wife doesn't seem to understand me, I still feel that catastrophizing about the end of human life on this planet is a valid concern. How can she not hear me and worry about the toilet paper supply?

When I'm arrogant, I insist my concerns are more important than anyone else's, and they should all share my worries. That doesn't go well for me, and walls go up. When I become humble, I realize that everyone feels strange right now, out of sorts, and frightened. Then I can connect with them. We become stronger, and our goals for any given day are more in line with each other.

Can there be a better example during these weird times of the helpfulness of humility over arrogance?

Can We Humbly Embrace Courage?

We intuitively think of a humble person as one who embraces audacity and arrogantly feels his/her mission is more virtuous than others. When a courageous person achieves victory in the quest, that person claims that the victory itself proves that the mission—and theirs alone—was blessed by God.

There's a humbler approach to being courageous that embraces love, compassion, and understanding of one's adversaries. To be truly courageous, we must accept the fact that losing is also part of the universe's plan.

Consider American sports, especially football. How many times after a big game or even an important touchdown do we see players and coaches thanking God for their victory? The humble approach would be to accept that when we face a big challenge, take an important exam, begin a game, or go into battle that defeat is just as likely, sometimes more so, than victory. Defeat is as much a part of the universal plan as victory. Humble courage allows us to accept the fact that defeat may be better for us and the world than victory.

It takes a lot of courage for me to admit that I failed my first attempt at the National Medical Board exam while in medical school. National Boards have three parts, all of which are required, along with at least one full year of post-medical school training, to obtain a license to practice medicine in the U.S. Without passing those Boards, a medical career becomes impossible.

When I learned I failed the first part of the Boards after weeks of intensive study and two years of basic science prep, I was crushed. I thought my dream of being a physician was over.

After two or three days of wallowing in self-pity and self-loathing, I realized that rather than giving up, I could suck it up, study, and take the exam again six months later. That was what I did. I realized I hadn't applied myself in test preparation. I wasn't properly rested or focused, and I wasn't in the best shape to expect victory.

I passed easily on my second attempt and went on to pass the other parts on schedule, ready to obtain the credentials necessary to be licensed to practice medicine in the United States.

Until that point, I was a good enough student to expect passage and usually got better than 90% on every exam. True, I studied hard, but I had an arrogance over my expectation of doing well. I wasn't so arrogant as to say that God blessed me with good grades, because I was somehow better or more talented than others.

Failing my first Board showed I wasn't better. I was a mere mortal. Going forward, I had to be more circumspect about my state of mind going into those exams. It took humility, and I didn't always achieve my desired result in future exams. That taught me there was something to be learned from defeat and failure. It ultimately made me a better physician and better man.

In these current days of pandemics, tumultuous politics, global climate change, crime, and financial uncertainty, along with calamities no one has yet considered, it takes courage just to get out of bed, walk out the front door, and face the day. It also takes humility. We must accept the fact that these horrible things could happen to any of us at any moment. If they do, they're as much a blessing as the positive outcomes. They're part of the tapestry of life on earth as human beings.

Humility also teaches that to be truly courageous, we must accept the fact that in competition, if we expect victory and feel we deserve it, we consider ourselves more blessed than those we hope to vanquish. The reality is that we're just people, and we have the same needs, desires, and hopes our opponents do. Winners and losers are connected through their sameness. Ironically, accepting and understanding the humanity and talents of our adversaries makes it more likely we'll achieve victory.

Some think courage involves overcoming fear to accomplish something we're afraid of. I differ with that. I believe courage involves accepting fear and doing what you must, anyway. There can be no courage without fear. Don't deny your fear or try to extinguish it. Face it, accept it, lean into it, and go forward, anyway, humbly and courageously.

The tens of thousands of healthcare workers on the front lines in the hospitals of New York and other major cities almost make me ashamed of the examples I offer of my own personal courage. The truth is, I struggle. I'm trained and have seen over thirty years of critical care, mainly for children in the intensive care unit. I have intubated hundreds of critically ill children, babies, and adolescents. I know how to run ventilators.

I'm also sixty-five-years old, a survivor of open-heart surgery, have controlled diabetes and hypertension, and the sole source of income for my family. The humble, courageous decision I had to make was to forego the opportunity to be on the front lines or the epicenter, trying to keep people alive until their lungs healed from COVID, and be honored as a hero who faces death to save lives. I stayed home to avoid dying.

It's not glamorous, but I have to believe, on some level, that it's courageous and honorable. Only time will tell if I made the right decision. My wife assures me of that every day. Due to my health risks, she won't let me leave the house except to walk the dog and tells me, "You have one duty in this family—to save YOUR Life!"

Sometimes, the humble, courageous choice isn't the most glamorous.

Gratitude During the Pandemic

Humbly Giving Thanks Every Day for Everything
New Age thinkers and wellness experts like Dr. Deepak Chopra have long recognized the life-affirming, health-giving aspects of gratitude. Dr. Chopra advocates a gratitude journal, where one spends some time each day listing the things for which one is thankful. This practice increases optimism. As one sticks with it, one finds the list grows, and things that were once not considered as gifts becomes things people are grateful for.

A recent article in *Psychology Today* discussed seven positive ways that embracing gratitude can result in greater mental and physical health.

Grateful people are less lonely, have more relationships, are physically healthier, exercise more, and visit the doctor regularly. Psychologically, gratitude acts as an antidote to negative emotions like resentment, envy, frustration, and regret. Taking a moment each day to be thankful for the positive things in one's life leads to greater self-esteem, and, therefore, more material success.

Athletes who are grateful and embrace "Thank you" as a common statement demonstrate improved mental clarity and performance.

Most importantly, gratefulness improves empathy and understanding of others, as if appreciating one's life leads to greater appreciation of the lives of others. That is a very important factor in the struggle of promoting humility to combat the separation of arrogance.

Conventional wisdom would have us believe that the arrogant think they are different and better, because they have more to be thankful for. In truth, the humble recognize everything in their lives is worth their thanks. The fact that we can open our eyes in the morning, take a breath, and think a clear thought deserves a moment of gratitude.

It has been suggested that the most-important and most-basic prayers are those of thanksgiving. Even intercessory prayers are authentic only if they begin with a moment of thanks.

Any journal is more successful if it begins with thoughts of thankfulness. Those who keep a gratefulness journal and are humble enough to be honest in those pages will enjoy boundless results in mental and physical positivity. Any wellness program should have gratefulness as its cornerstone, then move forward from there.

Deeprak Chopra recommends getting up each morning, opening the front door, noting three items in your field of view, and give thanks for them. It could be a bird singing in the tree in front of your house, the fragrance of the flowers blooming in the yard, the freshness of the air, or the greeting of a neighbor walking by with a pet on a morning constitutional.

The truly humble give thanks for the advancements of civilization they see, rather than grumbling about negatives. The folded newspaper on the walk deserves appreciation, for the culmination of civilization and intelligence that led to its production. Your automobile parked in the street in front of your house gives you the ability to transport your children, gets you to work, helps you visit friends, and allows you to purchase supplies for your family. All these should be the objects of our humble thanks.

Taking a moment each morning will grow into taking a little more time each day, as we begin to realize that everything in our field of view should humbly place us in awe of the miracle of being alive. Sooner or later, we realize that things, events, illnesses, and setbacks we see as negative have brought us something that makes us more-complete, empathetic, humble people. Make "Thank you" your most-frequent utterance, and the work will thank you for connecting.

Hope is an important element in surviving the latest challenge we face as Americans. The best way to engender and grow hope is through expressing and embracing gratitude. Whether it's Oprah's five things to be thankful for each day or Deepak's three things you see out your front door, taking a moment to be thankful for something in life breeds hope. Hope is the one emotion that can get us through the helplessness many feel.

To be truly thankful, one must be humble. Arrogance stands in the way of gratefulness, usually because the arrogant feel they are entitled to the good things in life. The humble see their lives as full of gifts for which they should be grateful. Such joyfulness leads to hope, and hope, as much as anything else, will see us through.

Sex and Gender—the Humble Approach

One positive development in cultural openness and progressive attitudes is our awareness and understanding of issues involving sexual preference and gender. During my lifetime as a typical baby boomer, I have seen dramatic changes in our attitude toward these issues.

When I was a kid, homosexuality was considered an anomaly and was a psychological disorder. To many, it was perversion, a lifestyle that could be chosen or suggested. People feared their children would come into contact with known homosexuals and felt it might be contagious, or that homosexual men would try to recruit children or molest them.

Thankfully, much of that has been dispelled, and our knowledge base, and our acceptance, have increased dramatically, reducing fear.

However, prejudice, bias, fear, and hate still exist due to the disconnection that comes from arrogance of seeing the differences between people rather than the similarities. Only those whose family members are homosexual, have open-mindedly embraced their own sexuality, have friends or colleagues who are LGBTQ, or are humbly open-minded about others can fully accept the fact that sexual preference is not a choice but is based on genetics and is already present at birth.

There is no clearer example of the fundamental contrast of humility vs. arrogance than the acceptance or rejection of those who differ from us sexually. Feeling such fundamental differences leads to disconnection, frequently to fear, and then the logical evolution of that fear into hate and violence, or hate crimes. One of the extremes of fear of the other and hate that results from feeling of difference was the tragic mass shooting at the Pulse nightclub in Orlando in the summer of 2016. Humility allows us to understand that sexuality is only one aspect of humanness. Essentially, we're the same. Feeling that allows us to empathize and connect, then to being able to love, protect, and nurture.

The transgender component of the LGBTQ tapestry presents particular challenges for those not willing to accept the similarities and embrace only the differences. Nothing is more troubling, confusing, and potentially depressing than trying to live in a body or an identity that doesn't feel like your own.

Many cases of suicide or severe clinical depression stem from those who identify with a different gender than the one in which they were born. Why are they depressed? It's the same reason as when a young man or woman comes out in a hetero-normative family that sees anything other than the 1950s version of the American family as abnormal, making them a threat to their own security. Those poor kids feel as if they're enemies of their families. Out of love, they choose to leave the family or even the earth to relieve themselves of the guilt of threatening their family's security.

Those who approach the issue of gender identity and sexuality with humility recognize the fact that there is a spectrum of gender and sexuality within all of us. We are born with it. There is nothing, no choice or cleansing program, that can change it. For many, such humility is difficult. Many people have spent their long lives within an extremely binary paradigm that is either male or female, and that person's sexual identity is consistent with his or her genitals. Such people prefer to only partner and have sex with members of the opposite sex. It takes a tremendous amount of self-examination, open-mindedness, and humility to accept that one may identify with a gender different than the one assigned at birth, or that one may fall in love and prefer to have sex with members of the same sex or opposite genders.

We live in enlightened times, where humility might actually be taking over, allowing us to accept those who don't look like we do, or to have relationships with those of any gender. It's no accident that, in 2020, we have been introduced to a presidential candidate who isn't only homosexual but who has been legally married to someone of the same sex. There is hope for the emergence of humility over arrogance, at least in gender and sexuality issues.

My teenagers continue to teach me. I recently attended a "gay" wedding. When I described it that way, my son asked, "Why do you call it a gay wedding? It's just a wedding."

He was right. I must still possess a bit of arrogant, separating, gender-binary identification, but I'm learning, and my humility allows me to do so.

Addiction—A Humble Approach?

Americans have become acutely aware of the ravages and societal expense of addiction in dealing with the opioid crisis. Many families deal with addicted or dependent individuals, not just as a result of opioid use but from addictions to alcohol, tobacco, food, sex, and other drugs.

There were periods in my life when I battled an unhealthy dependence on alcohol. I like to think that gave me an understanding of the difficulty and pain of dealing with that problem, not to mention the health risks. The definition of an alcoholic has long been elusive. The accepted definition for experts in addiction medicine is:

> Addiction is a treatable, chronic disease involving complex interactions among brain circuits, genetics, the environment, and an individual's life ex-

periences. People with addiction use substances or engage in behaviors that become compulsive and often continue despite harmful consequences. Prevention efforts and treatment approaches for addiction are generally as successful as for other chronic diseases.

ASAM Board of Directors,
September 15, 2019

For me, the key to understanding addiction continues within the context of this definition, is that the addicted individual continues to partake of the substance one is addicted to, despite experiencing negative consequences from the substance.

Substances or behaviors that lead to addiction involve invoking pleasure, stimulating the brain's pleasure centers with neurotransmitters like serotonin and dopamine to make one feel euphoric, and the intention to repeat the behavior. Substances like crack cocaine and methamphetamine, or behaviors like viewing pornography, are almost instantly addictive, calling people back for more after the first exposure.

Many people don't realize that behaviors like sexual activity, viewing pornography, or even compulsive shopping can become addicting by stimulating dopamine secretion in neuronal connections within the brain. We can better empathize with addicted individuals if we understand that any intensely pleasurable experience can become a compulsive behavior that can easily control one's life. In the extreme, the compulsion reaches a point where all other activities of daily living become secondary to the quest for the pleasurable activity. Alcohol is the easiest example to understand, especially for those of us who have battled with dependency.

In the depths of its control, I spent much of a normal day planning when I would have my first happy-hour vodka, wondering if I had an adequate supply, or worried I might be in a situation where I needed to have a serious conversation with someone. It didn't matter if the conversation was work-related or with a family member. My speech might be slurred from my second or third drink.

I woke up many mornings realizing I drank too much the previous night and probably took part in risky behaviors that left me ashamed, embarrassed, or both. I vowed never to drink again, realizing how unhealthy it was. By late afternoon, though, the cravings returned. I took the frosty bottle from the freezer, placed ice in a glass, and took my first sip with the self-deceived sense all was right with the world. I told myself I had control over my drinking. I could stop whenever I wanted, and I was too healthy for it to affect me.

Only after I suffered heart disease that required open-heart surgery, then a stroke, severe clinical depression, divorce, and damaged relationships with my children did I realize I needed help controlling my unhealthy relationship with alcohol. After working with an addiction therapist, for whom I will be forever grateful, I recovered, got healthy, and slowly developed a healthy relationship with alcohol, food, interpersonal relationships, and other dysfunctions in my life.

Humility arises from such situations. I understand and empathize with those for whom pleasurable experiences become compulsive ones that are difficult to control even when we know they're bad for us. Not only that, but a humble approach connects us by the realization that anyone can become addicted to a substance or activity that is unhealthy or might kill us. Arrogance separates us from those who struggle to break free of addiction, making us judgmental and uncompassionate. It makes us feel wrongly superior, as if we were better and could never become addicted to anything.

It can and does happen to anyone. That should humble us. The arrogant think of addicts as failed or weak, while they remain above the flaws that lead to addiction. They have no patience for those who are addicted and see no reason to spend time or resources in an attempt to help them.

It's not necessary to battle addiction in order to empathize humbly with those who struggle with substances or unhealthy activities. It is sufficient to recognize humbly that those who struggle with addiction are fundamentally no different than ourselves. We are all connected, and thus we are all in this together. When one person becomes addicted, we all are addicted, and we all need to be saved from the imprisonment of addiction.

PART FIVE

THE CORONAVIRUS PANDEMIC
A TIME FOR HUMILITY, NOT HUBRIS

CHAPTER 6

Spirituality

Oprah likes to say, "We are spiritual beings who live physical lives." Our physical being, with which we are overly obsessed, are simply vessels to transport our spirits during this particular phase of eternity while we're on the physical earth. It takes humility to accept that this life is just a phase, and our spiritual self, which we can't see in a mirror or find during surgery or medical school cadaver dissection, is the true center of our being.

I have discussed spiritual issues throughout this book, but I wanted to offer another paradigm within which to understand and humbly utilize spiritual issues. These are the major components of spirituality.

The Serenity Prayer is a work of genius and incorporates theology as well as the principles of humility to foster the connection and fulfillment many people espouse.

>Prayer for Serenity
>God grant me the serenity
>To accept the things I cannot change,
>The courage to change the things I can,
>And the wisdom to know the difference.
>Living one day at a time,

> Enjoying one moment at a time;
> Accepting hardship as a pathway to peace;
> Taking, as Jesus did,
> This sinful world as it is,
> Not as I would have it;
> Trusting that You will make all things right
> If I surrender to Your will;
> So that I may be reasonably happy in this life
> And supremely happy with You forever in the next.

When one looks at that prayer closely, serenity and humility seem almost to be synonymous and very closely interconnected with spirituality. There is acceptance and acknowledgement that hardship in life can actually be the pathway to peace. It also acknowledges our need and ability to improve what we can about ourselves and the world.

Spirituality requires taking the long view, giving up our arrogant sense that we can control everything, and being humble enough to recognize that if we optimize those things we can control in our lives, we might achieve reasonable happiness. Eternal happiness is something we can't even grasp as mortals.

Connectedness is important to spirituality in the sense that we are all connected at the soul level, guided by a power greater than ourselves. The foundation of the theory of the importance of humility is that it connects us to each other by our fundamental similarities, rather than arrogantly separating us by our differences.

The concept of miracles all around us accompanies the phrase of the prayer that we accept even hardship as a pathway to peace. I use a metaphor of feathers to represent the miracles in our lives. So much of recognizing miracles, which I define as messages or gifts from God, is being aware that if we open our eyes and notice them, they are everywhere. It's like finding our first feather on the ground. That makes us open to notice others, and we soon find them everywhere. That is something we realize by simply combining awareness with the acceptance that even unfortunate events in our lives can be miracles or pathways to peace.

Most important, we are best fulfilled in life if we humbly accept that our physical bodies are simply vessels for our spiritual or true selves.

Whether one chooses traditional Western Christianity, a more Eastern spirituality, early morning fishing, or a walk in the woods, the important thing for optimal fulfillment of the possibilities of life on earth, takes time to regularly recognize the fact that we, as human beings, are connected by our souls. There is a force greater than ourselves to guide us in the best method of caring for each other while inhabiting the planet. If you do that, you'll be glad you did.

Attachment—We Need Each Other

The science of attachment has been clearly elucidated. In the end, there is no question that we need each other. People require attachment to achieve well-bring and have any chance for fulfillment. Attachment behavior begins between parent and child immediately after birth. Its characteristics are often reflected in people's relationships with others throughout their lives.

There are four basic forms of attachment, as described by Bowlby in the 1950s:

Secure—autonomous; secure

Avoidant—dismissing; suspicious

Anxious—preoccupied, suspicious

Disorganized; unresolved, unsuccessful

The kind of attachment a child forms with its parents is adaptive, in the sense that the child reacts to the perceived relationship with its caregiver, doing so in a way to protect itself from the pain of rejection, or, in the extreme, abuse.

As older children and adults, humility is necessary to recognize that the success or failure of our relationships is the result of the relationship we had with our parents as infants. The die is cast early. Not all hope is lost, though. We can cognitively improve our relationships by humbly recognizing the patterns of the way we get along with others are acutely established in our early years.

Secure attachment is the most successful and one we aspire to achieve. If infants feel secure in relying on their parents' presence and caregiving, they will grow up thinking that those relationships, and other close ones, will always be there.

Insecure attachment with parents results when infants and children are never sure their parents will be there for them. This phenomenon results from several factors, with abuse and neglect the most obvious.

When a child is fearful of its parents or isn't confident what kind of reception it will receive, an insecure attachment results. Even parents who mock, ridicule, or make jokes about their children can make the children feel insecure about their attachment to their parents. These individuals go through life having great difficulty forming secure relationships with other adults. They struggle to find happiness and fulfillment.

Babies who can count on their parents to be there when needed, to feed them when hungry, protect them when frightened, and comfort them when they are lonely, will always associate their parents with safe, secure, warm, dry spaces. When they form relationships later in life, particularly with their life partners, they know they can count on the same things.

Children who are ignored, neglected, ridiculed, or abused won't securely attach to their caregivers. Later in life, they will have difficult forming secure relationships.

According to Dr. Bowlby, there are three forms of insecure attachment. The avoidant attacher is wary of any kind of relationship, always expecting and predicting that it will go poorly at some point. They expect to be disappointed and refuse to get too close to anyone. They become unsuccessful at forming any kind of attachment.

An anxious attacher forms successful relationships but puts them at risk by being apprehensive. That kind of insecurity can be challenging to a successful relationship. I have had a fair amount of experience with that. I formed many anxious attachments. It is a challenging experience that usually results in unsuccessful relationships.

Then there is the person who forms disorganized attachments. That can be someone who unsuccessfully connected with his or her parents for any of a number of reasons. That attachment behavior is recapitulated in their adult relationships, preventing them from connecting with others. The sociopath, or anyone unable to express empathy or compassion for anyone other than themselves, would be at the extreme end of that category.

For someone who has had difficulty forming successful relationships throughout life, it helps to accept humbly there may be contributing reasons for that deficiency in life that stem from difficult relationships in infancy. The answer is to avoid blaming everyone and instead seek help. One must find a therapist who can help figure out a strategy for relationships. The person must understand that having such a background doesn't rule out successful relationships. Understanding one's personal emotional development may help someone work productively to improve and optimize his existing relationships.

To blame others arrogantly and avoid insight that might come from psychological assistance accomplishes nothing.

Why attachment?

The main premise behind this book—that humility connects, and meekness leads to inheriting the earth—relies on attachment science. People need to be connected to one another. To do that, we need humbly to accept our similarities, including the fact that we are products of our emotional pasts. We can use that as connective tissue, as opposed to the assumed uniqueness and differences that drive us apart. We need attachment to survive. Humility fosters attachment, while arrogance inhibits it.

Let's Take a Walk

In my book *The Alive Five* (2013), I outlined the five things every family can do to live healthier, happier lives. The second aspect is to take part in one hour of activity or exercise each day. My favorite way to satisfy that was what I called, the Won Hour Walk. I used "won," because the advantages of the activity win a lot for your life.

All the numbers about calories, steps, and time point out the beauty of walking for one hour. The average person, walking at a comfortable pace, moves at three to four miles per hour. On average, one mile covers 2,500 steps. Four miles takes the fabled 10,000 steps, a distance prescribed by many as a minimum number to ensure good health. If we calculate that one mile burns approximately 100 calories, then 400 calories per day results in a caloric burn of about 3,000 calories each week. Given typical metabolic rates, that results in one pound of weight loss each week. It's easy to calculate the math for longer periods of time.

There are far-greater benefits than just weight management, although that is vitally important. Still, it might not help you to feel good in the moment.

For me, walking is a meditative experience, even if I'm listening to the news or *Broadway* on XMSerious radio. It could be the rhythm of the steps, the coordination with breathing, or the focus on the task without having to be concerned about outside worries.

Clearing the mind, which is typically challenging for people who try traditional meditation, is far easier when one is strolling down the road in a neighborhood, walking down a busy Manhattan street, or placidly strolling through the woods while enjoying the sights, sounds, and smells all around.

Even when walking with someone a person cares about, the meditative and connective qualities can be profound.

I want to take my readers on a sample walk through a typical American neighborhood. I will guide people through the meditative moments that are possible while moving through one hour.

You wake up feeling fairly content, knowing you're not operating at full capacity until your first cup of coffee, which you brew. Savor each aspect of it. Let the fragrance of freshly brewed coffee waft through the air to your nostrils, awakening your senses. Sip it slowly, letting the first sip nearly scald your tongue and lips, while each subsequent sip is slightly cooler and ready to be digested. It slides down your throat, warming you and the entire length of your esophagus. When it reaches your stomach, you can almost feel the effects of the coffee, as the hot, black nectar is absorbed through your stomach lining.

You begin to wake up.

You realize you should meditate, but you settle for a few moments of peaceful contemplation before going outside. When you're in a good, receptive state, you adjust your shoes and go out.

Cool air strikes your face. At first, you gasp, then breathe slowly and deliberately, in and out, concentrating on relaxation and nurturing your tissues with oxygen on inhalation, ridding your body of carbon dioxide and tension when you exhale. Any initial muscle stiffness vanishes, and you feel relaxed. Whatever tension you may have had earlier drains out of your body through the soles of your feet into the giant reservoir of the earth.

Your attention goes to the sounds around you. The birds, once a disorganized cacophony, sound like a symphony, and you marvel at the beauty of the natural world all around. It feels life-affirming.

You continue at a comfortable pace, not concentrating on the time spent or the time remaining but instead on the rhythm and comfort. Your muscles become loose and warm, your body doing what it's designed to do, a task you've been doing without thinking since sometime around your first birthday.

You enjoy the rest of your walk, praising yourself to make yourself do it every day for the rest of your life as an affirmation and celebration.

Arrogance and the Death of Truth

It has often been said, particularly in the age of Trump, that although we are entitled to our own opinions, we aren't entitled to our own facts. In this age, we have experienced the coining of the term "fake news," the entire concept of which may be fake.

We went through an impeachment process that hinged entirely on two different interpretations, and thus narratives, of the same facts.

At this writing, we are deep into the Democratic primaries of the 2020 election and the early stages of the COVID-19 coronavirus outbreak and possible pandemic. This later became a certainty. Under these circumstances, as well as the foreign and domestic crises we face regularly, the truth is essential for families to make the right decisions about the safety and security of their family members.

In a video of Trump in a conference room with leaders of the pharmaceutical industry, he asked one particular leader, "When will a vaccine be available against COVID-19?"

"It will take about two months to have a vaccine prototype ready for initial trials."

"Oh, good. Two months, then. I like that."

"Two months to phase one trials," the executive said.

"OK. Two months, then. I like that."

Even after the industry representative explained that phase one trials lead to more trials, and it will take a year to eighteen months before a vaccine is ready for widespread public use, Trump still follows his own narrative.

"I like two months better," he said. "Let's just say two months."

That gives a glimpse into how Trump's narrative, which is often far from reality, takes hold. In a way, these are insidious lies that take on a grain of truth or are part of a fundamental misunderstanding. Steven Colbert called this "truthiness." It's a nugget that has the air of truth but won't stand up to scrutiny or fact checking.

People have bias, something that makes them believe statements that fit their underlying narrative or theory of how the world works. Many such paradigms turn out to be conspiratorial and politically driven.

Why do people do this? There are several explanations. The available heuristic is a mental shortcut, where people believe certain facts that help them reach conclusions they already hold and are convenient explanations for things they don't understand but require the least amount of work or research to verify. Such mental laziness is also human nature.

The principle of conformational bias pushes people to believe something that already fits into their notions of how things work. If people believe that Democrats, Russians, Republicans, or Martians are trying to control their thoughts and actions, then any fact people don't understand or haven't researched themselves can be explained away as a conspiracy.

Some people, who don't readily accept lies, also make the mistake that they can change people's minds by arguing facts. The truth is that once such untruths are embedded into people's consciousness, they are difficult, if not impossible, to remove.

Pervasive untruths are a stubborn weed in the mental garden. The roots are usually so deep they can't be pulled out, even with garden tools and chemicals. The only way to remove a stubborn mistruth is by tearing up the garden and starting over.

Humility enters into several stages of this process. People must humbly listen to all the facts presented, do their own homework, and embrace that which is based on research, provable, and, sometimes, inconvenient. People owe it to themselves to realize humbly that not everything they hear, even from others they trust, is true. People can more easily connect with others if they vow to pass on only facts, opinions, or notions they have heard only if, like the best reporters of older newspapers, they have confirmation from trusted sources.

The Ego Hates Humility

There are many definitions of the word "ego," but in common vernacular, it equates with one's sense of self. Within it is a sense of honesty, boundaries, agency, and esteem. There is also self-protection. People with strong egos, who find it difficult to see the blending of their self with others, see others as a threat to their integrity, safety, and identity.

While the concept of humility, which states we are connected by our similarities and can inherit the earth by acknowledging that—may threaten those with an unhealthy egocentricity, humility can actually strengthen the ego of those with a secure sense of self and improve one's esteem and security. This demonstrates that we are stronger and better when connected to others.

Those with unhealthy egos, who some call narcissistic, believe they are the center of the universe. Every human relationship is important only to the extent that it affects them personally or can create a result of their impact on others. There is no sense of empathy. The only acknowledgment of anyone other than themselves is a threat.

Those with healthy egos, who have realized the importance of inheriting the earth, have boundaries but see them as welcoming border crossings with security and openness. Connecting to others, particularly on a spiritual level, adds to and deepens one's sense of self, expanding these people's impact on the world.

Arrogant people see personal boundaries as a Trumpian Wall. They must never let someone get too close, because those people are threats who will violate someone's ego safety. There is an exception, however. An arrogant individual may appear humble by letting someone get close, but that is a trick. The arrogant person has calculated that such behavior makes them appear humbler and therefore better people. The arrogant person sees that being perceived that way can sometimes get more for their own benefit. That isn't humility. It's completely egocentric and the epitome of arrogance, not to mention being fundamentally dishonest.

As with many such issues surrounding humility and arrogance, the key to a fulfilled life is to strike a balance, being neither completely humble nor completely arrogant but a bit of both. This optimizes the ego, the sense of self, and one's security. When one is in conflict or feels detached, disconnected, and alone, one should bend toward humility, since that approach connects and promotes empathy.

Although humility connects us with others by recognizing our similarities, that isn't always safe. The reality is there are evil people with whom it is unsafe and even impossible to connect. That is true of sociopaths, psychopaths, and incorrigible criminals. We must remain safe from such individuals, so that we are encouraged to make humble connections with those who can enrich us and whom we can enrich in turn through our connections.

The ego is with everyone. It can act to protest, promote, or nurture us when handled thoughtfully. If arrogance guides the ego's development, people will end up making decisions that promote their own egos at the expense of others', leading to disconnection. If our egos allow us to form connections humbly by acknowledging the relative value of others who aren't like us, our lives will increase in value to others and to the greater good.

Humility at the End of Life

Most people consider death, especially of a loved one, as one of the worst things that can happen. I wish to share some personal experiences as both a physician and family member.

My book *Moondance to Eternity* focused on my experiences at the bedside of kids facing life-threatening illnesses and death. While these events were centered around something devastating and tragic, in each story of sick kids and their families was a moment of absolute triumph, peace, or a gift.

I won't call it arrogance per se, but because we have a fundamental fear of death, mainly based on ignorance of what it looks like, it's definitely not like what's in movies or TV. Humility enters the picture by accepting that knowledge empowers us and lessens our fears, making it easier to accept the reality that we are all going to die.

My father, an old man in his late eighties after a long, successful life, died of complications of Parkinson's Disease and bladder cancer during a tropical storm that swept over north Florida. Partly because he could be sheltered and still have basic utilities, and because my mother wasn't ready for him to die at home, he spent his last night in a local hospice facility. She was with him, as she had been during sixty-three years of marriage, when he drew his last breath. When she feels low or is a little desperate, she remembers how hard it was to watch him struggle for his last breaths, and how awful it was to feel the warmth drain from his body to be replaced by the cold finality of death.

When she steps back, humbly recognizing she did all she could for him during his entire life, she remembers their last kiss. As she described it, he hadn't opened his eyes for a while nor responded to her voice, but, when she leaned over to kiss his lips, knowing it was probably for the last time, he responded by puckering his lips and reflexively kissing her back, as he'd done thousands of times before. That moment was a gift she will always cherish. She would not have recognized it or been ready for it had she not, in those last moments, accepted the reality of his death and celebrated the lifelong love they shared.

She has strong religious faith, holding in her heart a concrete view of heaven and the afterlife. Partly due to the fact of her humble acceptance of her husband's death, combined with the faith that, after death, something better awaits, and her humble acceptance of the reality of life, she no longer fears death. She even jokes about wondering how she'll recognize my father and the other family members who have passed once she gets there. I find strength in her faith and confidence. This strength was only bolstered by her sharing every moment with her husband, including his death.

It's not necessary to embrace organized, traditional, Western Christianity to accept humbly the reality of death. In general, all organized religions center around the principle of explaining the reality that we alone, among the other organisms on earth, live our lives knowing that they will end. Some utilize fantastic, almost crazy explanations for death and the afterlife.

The common denominator of all religion, something in the hearts of those who live their lives without the human fear of death is the knowledge that, when this life ends, and the inevitable moment of our demise occurs, it will be all right. As I age, fighting chronic illness and the possibility of a worldwide pandemic, I try to spend a moment during my morning meditation accepting the fact that I will die, and it will be all right.

I'm not on the front lines as many physicians are, dealing with those who are ill and dying from the coronavirus pandemic. I often lament that, but I am also aware of the horror for the thousands of families and victims of the virus so far. Sadly, the arrogance involved in the idea that it won't happen to them, as seen in Trump, Boris Johnson, and other world leaders, has only made the pandemic worse. Trump tells us that the pandemic will go away, and the numbers will fall to zero, while Johnson brags about how he still shakes hands with everyone. All people have a fear of death and the pervasive arrogance that it won't happen to us.

Those who are living within the confines of their homes, wearing masks in public, sending only the healthiest person out to buy groceries no more than once a week, and trying to generate income from whatever sources they can find, are somehow also able to find the humility to keep ourselves as safe as possible while being responsible for the health of those we meet.

I walked Snickers, the Wonder Dog, around the neighborhood for all the years I have lived here, greeting people as we pass, sometimes within a few feet of each other. Now Snickers and I have to cross to the other side of the street and not pass people too closely on the sidewalk. If the other person and I don't have masks, we nod hello without exhaling, and try to smile with our eyes.

We do that out of respect for the coronavirus. We're humble enough to know it could kill any one of us and will do so slowly, inexorably, and horribly. It is still a mystery why our leaders lack that humility. Without it, they don't connect with the rest of us, and they can't understand the reality of the deadly nature of the disease the virus causes.

We will only be saved from this horrible virus—which seems likely to continue for a while—if we reject arrogance and denial and humbly accept the realities of the death that comes from infection via the coronavirus. Thinking that the virus will avoid us if we're White, rich, young, healthy, Republican, and Christian is arrogant and will become a deadly game when loved ones are taken to the hospital to become sick and die.

There is another unique problem with this pandemic. We can't even properly mourn those who have died. Relatives can't sit at the bedside of dying family members. Without mourning, those deaths can't be processed. Grief will combine with regret, and the psychological damage, particularly for the healthcare workers who act as family members for the dying, will continue for a generation.

Humbly Accept Aging

Everyone is getting older. I will soon face my sixty-fifth birthday, which brings Social Security, Medicare, and many other things, and I might be aging faster than many others. If not faster, then perhaps I'm aging further, but still, everyone is getting older. At some point, we must face our own mortality and have a strategy in place to deal with that without letting it drive us insane. If we are not careful, the futility of life will become a form of arrogance. The fact that we being dying the moment we are born is too much for some. Depending on whether a person approaches that fact with humility or arrogance affects whether that person sees imminent death as depressing or an opportunity to do one's best.

It all goes back to the Serenity Prayer. We must pray for the knowledge to see the things we can change and those we cannot. People can change things in their lifestyle to make them healthier and happier, as mentioned in *The Alive Five*. However, no one has the power to change the inevitability of death. The trick is to accept and find peace in knowing that death is part of God's will and is, therefore, good by definition. We must strive for the intelligence to realize that death is the one thing everyone faces and no one can change.

What we can control is what we do with our lives during the limited time we are on earth. We have a role in our relationships, the work we do, the art we create, and the way we raise our children.

When I first mentioned the Serenity Prayer, I called attention to the phrase, *Accepting hardship as a pathway to peace*. That may be one of the most-beautiful yet least-known and least-understood notions in the long version of the prayer. Part of spirituality is accepting the hardships in life as gifts or miracles, the purpose of which may not be immediately understood. As part of the big picture, though, they are necessary parts of the master plan for the universe. The most-obvious hardship people face is the fact that everyone grows old, develops some form of age-related illness, deteriorates, and dies. Being able to access that as a pathway to peace should be a goal for all, yet it requires humility.

Earlier in this book was a discussion on how arrogance connotes control. Humility requires acceptance of the Serenity Prayer and that there are some things people can control, but there are many other aspects over which people have no control at all.

What does that look like? How can we accept aging and the inevitability of death with grace and joy?

We must start with gratitude. When we wake up each day, our first prayer should be to thank God and the universe for the blessing of our first breath, the loved ones around us, our health, and the optimism we can share.

If someone has a traditional nine-to-five job, he or she should relish it. We should enjoy the people with whom we work and notice how our own work contributes to society, our family, our friends, and our neighborhood and community.

If people are retired or in transition, they should take stock in the fact that, until their last breath, they are still contributing, teaching, counseling, loving, nurturing, and making the planet a better place than they found it. That's our job as humans.

Forbes magazine has a special called *50 over 50,* recognizing the contribution of artists, entrepreneurs, and all those who shape society yet may be forgotten, because they have grown old.

I'm in that group with all the other seniors. Still, we must do whatever we can with our slightly less-efficient bodies. Even our physical potential can be optimized by taking good care of ourselves, eating healthy foods, and being sure we have people to care about who care about us. We must humbly accept that as long as we're alive, our work isn't yet done.

CHAPTER 7

Reacting to the Pandemic

At the time of this writing, the world stands on the precipice of an unprecedented pandemic. As the economy crumbles, store shelves empty, and people lock themselves in their homes, hoping they don't end up in an understaffed, under-equipped hospital. We are also learning that human reaction to an epidemic may hurt us worse than the actual disease. What are our choices? How can we face those choices humbly?

Humility is needed over arrogance, because the connection that comes with humility is more necessary now than ever before. Ironically, at a time when we need each other more than perhaps any other time in history, we are expected to remain socially isolated and keep a safe distance from everyone, including family.

There are scientific, medical, sociological, psychological, emotional, and economic issues to consider. All are connected by the current threat to humanity.

Medically and scientifically, there is little doubt that we face an epidemic. It comes from the corona category of viruses, called COVID-19, and it is characterized by the usual unspecific symptoms of any respiratory viral infection. We can only differentiate this virus from the influenza or other viral infections that are common to the same time of year by specific testing. The tests aren't always available, and thus far, they require excessively stringent testing criteria. The more people we test, the more likelihood we have of discovering the true extent of the infection, which would define the "denominator" of the epidemiological equation.

As the epidemic worsens, the shift moves from test to treatment, and that creates a major crisis point, because hospital staff will face an overwhelming need for beds, personnel, and equipment. We aren't prepared for that.

The clinical aspects of the illness are horrific, as survivors and caretakers have explained. We are beginning to understand there is a broad spectrum to the disease that results from COVID-19. The respiratory disease progresses from a dry cough to chest discomfort to shortness to breath to dramatically low oxygen levels, then it can lead to coma and respiratory failure and death.

Those who make it to the hospital are typically intubated and placed on mechanical ventilators. My dear friend and colleague, Dr. Harvey Friedman, an experienced pulmonologist in Chicago, says the respiratory failure and severity of the illness are like something he has ever seen. Patients don't respond to traditional therapies, and they very quickly progress to intubation and ventilators before dying. The worst part is that they face this illness alone. When they die, they are sometimes witnessed by families on iPads or iPhones. Dr. Friedman said it was harder on the families than the patients, who were thankfully heavily sedated while being intubated.

Combine that with the fact that many of the caretakers are exposed to a heavy viral load and face the possibility of illness and death, and the pandemic becomes a terribly tragedy. It makes the discussion on the need to approach the inevitability of death humbly even more poignant and applicable. These times require existential discussions among ourselves and our families.

Concerning the economy, anything tied to the stock market will vanish first, then businesses will close, and products and services will become less available. That's when we need to come together as a people to take care of ourselves, our families, and each other. Perhaps that will be the finest moment of the crisis. In times of crisis, humanity is often at is best. Humbly accepting reality and knowing we must do our best to help others will accentuate our greatness. I have faith in all of us.

At the end, when the epidemic finally wanes, there may be one million dead, maybe two. We might all come to know someone who dies from COVID-19. It will forever change our history and will become an inflection point, like the world wars, 9/11, and major hurricanes. I believe we are at our best when coming through such national and worldwide crises. Then the rebuilding can begin. We must use whatever money we have to support businesses, buy products, and hire services.

We will survive, and we will be better for having gone through this.

In the midst of it, though, what do we do now? How should we behave? How do we plan for our families?

It was my teen daughter who reminded me that we should worry only about the things we control. She recited her own version of the Serenity Prayer. We can't control the existence of the virus, its worldwide effects, or even the crashing economy.

We can heed suggestions by the government and our public health officials, or we can ignore them and accept the consequences. We can attend to our personal hygiene, avoid crowds, wash our hands, clean surfaces, and, most importantly, stay home. We can even avoid the lines and crowds at the grocery store by having supplies delivered, a crucial step during the stay-at-home period.

If we or someone we know becomes ill, we must humbly accept it was outside our control. We give them the care we can offer and hope for the best. Even with that, we must accept there could be bad outcomes, suffering, and sacrifice.

As I wrote earlier, even these things are gifts and potential miracles from which we will be better afterward. This could be our finest hour.

Crisis Talk with Children

After a week of electing to stay home, leaving the house only for groceries, meds, and even the liquor store, we fell into a routine. After our morning foraging activities, we caught up with the news on the

TV from my computer, watching incessant cable news coverage of the evolving coronavirus pandemic. Death tolls rose, medical equipment became scarce, there was no lodging for the homeless, and general uncertainty.

"The media is just so negative," my son said.

"The facts are quite negative," I replied. "They have to report the facts."

In Gen Z terms, he replied, "But they're just so dramatic!"

That began one of the more-meaningful conversations we enjoyed since being homebound. It was therapeutic for both of us. I learned that teens want to know the facts, but that's all. The political discourse, arguments over policy, and references to history are beyond their scope of interest.

It was very similar to the viewpoint of young children. The experts say that the best way to deal with the youngest among us as anxiety rises during a crisis is honesty and not too much information. We should answer the questions they ask but keep it specific, with a minimum of emotionalism.

If your youngest asks, "Mommy, Jason told me we're all going to die of a virus. Are we?"

Your answer should have compassion and then a specific question. "I can tell you're frightened by this. That's OK. Do you know what a virus is?"

Then, very clearly and concisely, we must explain, using our own experience as a starting point. Parents should ask if their child remembers the last time he or she had a cold or tummy ache and had to stay home from school. Explain that it was due to a virus, and most viruses cause problems that go away quickly, although some people can become very sick.

A mother might add, "Mommy is staying home from work, and you're home from school, to make sure you don't get too sick."

Another thing to add would be to say that very smart doctors and scientists are working on medicines to protect everyone. Those will help us get well quickly.

As parents, we must speak calmly and not let worry or fear creep into our voices. Everyone has moments of concern, depression, and even anger during such times, but those discussions should be kept with one's significant other, a journal, a close friend, or a therapist.

If someone wishes to contact us, Drs. John and Lisa, we would love to talk. We can be reached through drsjohnandlisa.com or drjohnandlisa.com. We receive email at drjohnmonaco@yahoo.com

Above all, we must remember that humility is always important for all of us, including ourselves, our spouses, and our older children. We should recite the Serenity Prayer and reflect on it.

On Easter Sunday, my wife asked me to say grace. All I could think of was to comment briefly that the best path to hope is through gratitude, so we should all reflect on that for which we feel grateful, and then hope would germinate.

We should remind our families there are things we can control, like keeping food and water available, observing good hygiene, washing our hands, and cleaning all surfaces. The *Alive Five* can be observed during these shutdown periods in the pandemic while people are confined to their homes. That can be extremely helpful and will keep us in good health and good spirits.

As taught by the Serenity Prayer, there is much that is God's will and out of our control. The nature of the virus at the heart of the pandemic is communicability and pathology. We must humbly seek the wisdom to know the difference between the things we can control and those we can't. If we can see that, we will find peace, and our children will sense our serenity and feel comforted.

Alive Five in a Crisis
Humbly Maintaining Control

The world is in uncharted waters due to the global coronavirus pandemic. Much of the time, people feel out of control. They don't know how long they'll be encouraged or forced to remain at home. People wonder, *What if we get sick? Will there be resources for us? What about our friends and family members?*

People feel torn between the self-centered need to protect themselves and their loved ones and the intrinsic altruism within all to do what is best for their community and the world. One example is hoarding toilet paper, but buying more than someone needs risks adding to a shortage that is bad for everyone else.

People tend to overbuy when they worry about shortages. Feeding their families is something people feel they can control. The pandemic and its effects present the most-obvious real-world example of the Serenity Prayer most will ever experience in their lifetimes. Perhaps that is one of the lessons people are meant to learn from the experience.

The Serenity Prayer asks God to give us the strength to change the things we can, the courage to let go of the things we can't change, and the wisdom to know the difference.

What should everyone do? One option is to follow the tenets of *The Alive Five*, a book I wrote. Those five elements are:

1. Family meals
2. Activity/exercise
3. Avoiding processed sugar
4. Promoting fruits and vegetables
5. Embracing mindfulness

One of the elements of family meals is planning, buying, and preparing the meals. While shopping during the pandemic, we teach our children about necessities and the concept of sufficiency while protecting supplies for others.

One of the only reasons we can responsibly leave our homes is to go to the grocery store for supplies, including paper products. For a small family of two or three individuals, that can be an opportunity to have a change of scenery. Dr. Lisa, my wife, who was blessed with the homecraft gene unlike the rest of us, fashioned designer surgical masks for all of us. She plans to make those available for local hospitals, too.

Since we started staying at home, food has become our focus. Shopping, preparing, and eating as a family keeps our collective health and the health of others in mind. It also gives us an opportunity to consider recipes that would benefit large groups or people who live in areas of scarcity.

Numbers three and four on the list concentrate on fruits and vegetables and avoiding added sugar. Those principles can be observed as a family during mealtimes.

Number two is the exercise or activity component. People are permitted to leave home for exercise or dog walking. That can be a lovely time for individuals and families. People wisely keep their distance during such times. The humble understand, while the arrogant influencers in politics and opinionated media don't. The humble are compliant, willing to protect themselves and their families while also altruistically trying to protect each other.

The final, and possibly the most-important, element is being mindful. It means more than being mindful about eating and activities, which was the original intent of *The Alive Five*. In addition, we should be mindful about the implications of the lessons of this important period of world history.

During a pandemic, the struggle between self-preservation and altruism is the central issue. There is grasping with the country's role in a world that isn't separated by borders but by collections of endemic nodes. Ultimately, this forms the juxtaposition of humility and arrogance. The humble realize there is no difference between people from various parts of the world. The vulnerability to death and illness is universal. The arrogant will take a one-man-for-himself attitude, while the humble will pitch in to help all.

Not enough can be said for the ER and ICU nurses and physicians who are at the front lines of the battle. Health, age, and other reasons prevent us from being with them, fighting the pandemic shoulder-to-shoulder. That gives us pause and more than a little guilt and shame. Still, we can be there in other ways, whether it's consoling and informing readers and listeners or finding other practical modalities that can be used when the pandemic is over to contribute our years of medical and pediatric experience.

Whatever someone's professional situation may be, it will be a difficult time for everyone. People need to help each other and be honest and forthright about their strengths and weaknesses. It's a time for meditation, prayer, vulnerability, and availability. We should be there for each other, leading with kindness, compassion, love, and humility. We can and will get through this, and we'll be even better for it.

Life after COVID-19—Distancing Forever?

As of 4/13/20, nearly 105,000 people have died from the coronavirus infection, including almost 22,000 Americans. There will be many more. When the virus finally runs its course through her immunity or immunization, those who survive—which will be most of us—will face a world that has been permanently changed. People will be wary of congregating in large numbers for any reason. When and if sports starts up again, there will be no live audiences for a while. people will watch sports events on TV and cheer for their teams in small family or friend groups.

We must face the future humbly, realizing that, while our personal quality of life is important, the health of others and society is also our responsibility.

The way we practice medicine will be forever changed, too. I suspect that telehealth and telemedicine will become standard patient care for many practices. There will be a surge in concierge practices, too. Since potential patients will be understandably reluctant to leave their homes, physicians will need to meet them where they live. The advantage to telehealth is that caregivers won't have to touch their patients, although performing procedures will certainly require human contact. With the advent of AI and robotics, even that may require less close human contact than before.

It's ironic that what has been missing in the physician-patient encounter over the last few years is that the patient feels less connected to the provider. The provider spends less time with each patient due to economic pressures, and the encounter has become encumbered by computers, which require the provider's time to fill in the medical record.

In a good telemedicine model, the provider gives the patient his/her undivided attention, with the two of them face-to-face, looking directly at each other, paying close attention to the other's words. Perhaps more-accurate information exchange will occur.

The most-important aspect of the doctor-patient encounter is the history, the way the patient describes his illness and state of health. It's also the most-important part of a physical exam. The benefit of telemedicine is the emphasis on history over the need to examine the patient physically.

In pediatrics, where I spent over thirty year of my professional life, most of what is needed to be learned to arrive at an accurate diagnosis and provide an effective treatment plan comes from interviewing the patient and parent, then to visually examine the child. In an ambulatory setting, the first and most-important question is, "Is the child sick or well?" Next is, "Should the child be admitted to the hospital, or can he or she be treated as an outpatient?"

Those questions are answered in large part during the first few minutes of the encounter, through history and visual inspection of the child's state of well-being. All of that can be done without touching the patient.

If the patient needs to be examined physically, arrangements can be made. The follow-up from the initial exam could be done concierge style in the patient's home, where a more-accurate picture of the patient's life, family, and surroundings can be ascertained. That presents another major change in the traditional healthcare model.

Some among the medical community will arrogantly refuse to accept such radical changes. If they can't set their arrogance aside and humbly accept that we must learn from the pandemic, survive it, and grow, it was all for naught. Converting to telemedicine and telehealth will take humility, which I maintain is our most-important survival characteristic.

The 2020 Election
Arrogance: A Matter of Life and Death

Does American exceptionalism actually mean American arrogance or hubris? Is Trump emblematic of that flow? Can we survive if he is re-elected? The one bright spot in the coronavirus pandemic, the symbolic ceremonial signing of the pandemic relief bill, was undertaken in the Oval Office with only Republicans present. That is combined with Trump's rise in the polls as people are dying throughout the country. What explains that disconnect? More importantly, can the country move past it?

I still have hope we can. Never before in my lifetime has it been more obvious that elections have consequences, and the presidency is truly important for all citizens of America.

In the first part of this book, I explained how Trump was both a cause and a result of our current culture of arrogance, and how, to survive and achieve personal and societal fulfillment, it is imperative that we embrace humility. That trait will ultimately bring us together, while arrogance separates us more and more.

Since before his presidency began, Trump has ruled by the separation that comes from arrogance. It has only gotten worse since. Now that we are on the precipice of biological extinction and/or economic ruin, his arrogance has only gotten worse, and so has our separation, anxiety, and misery.

It is no cosmic accident that, at the peak of this global pandemic, where the survival of the earth's population is at stake, we will be holding the most-important election of our lives.

This one will be crucial and might represent life and death. It may already be too late. Only time will tell, but we must turn away from such arrogance and from a man who stared into the eclipse when experts advised against it. Trump first told us that the Russian involvement was a hoax, then that the coronavirus was a hoax. He has refused to provide ventilators to governors who don't "appreciate" him.

If such dangerous behavior isn't obvious to American voters, I can't imagine what more it will take. Luckily, he passed the coronavirus relief plan, probably because it would cost him votes if he refused.

He has discounted the advice of doctors and experts, because he doesn't feel they're right, or that it suits him. He denies good science and rejected the need for early detection and intervention when the virus was still in central China. He calls it the "China" virus.

When the worldwide Ebola epidemic, and possible pandemic, threatened to leave West Africa and come to the United States, President Obama sent a team to West Africa, where the outbreak was contained. Still, hospitals throughout America prepared for the appearance of Ebola patients at their door. PPEs first were noticed by average Americans during that period.

With the coronavirus, Trump relied on borders and the distance from China to protect us. Separateness and arrogance have been his allies and control his attitude toward dealing with issues he has faced in his presidency.

At the moment, the leading opposition candidate and most likely the Democratic nominee is Joe Biden. By the time this book is published, the election may be essentially over. I hope the American public and the electoral college do the right thing. Former Vice President Biden is the picture of humility and empathy, the polar opposite of the personality of Trump and his minions. Not only is Biden quick to describe and own his personal tragedies and imperfections, he connects with others through his humility, combined with his experience in dealing with health crises and pandemics, not to mention the economic collapse of 2008. He easily shows he is the right candidate.

History may record that Trump brought the pandemic to America, or at least made it worse. With his hubris and arrogance, he accelerated its spread and is responsible for thousands if not millions of American deaths. This pandemic is the worst since the 1918 flu. Given our technological advances in the last 100 years, this is ironic and tragic.

We must do the right thing by electing the humble candidate and saving lives.

Humbly Accepting the Pandemic

The only hope we have of surviving the pandemic intact is by approaching it humbly, not arrogantly thinking we're invulnerable. The worldwide aspect of the infection points out that no one is exempt. As human beings, we're alike in our vulnerability to this virus. It doesn't care about rich or poor, Black or White, urban or rural, male or female, old or young, Democrat or Republican. All are equally vulnerable. The virus needs a human host to survive. As long as there are people living on the planet, the virus will find them. That thought alone should make us humble.

There are several lines of defense, but all require a humble approach. Our only hope for regaining a meaningful life is through humility. We can see that by tracing the origins of the pandemic in the United States.

We first heard about cases of this virus in Wuhan, China. The arrogant Trump administration dismissed it as a Chinese virus, stating our borders would protect us. When that wasn't enough, the borders were closed to anyone from China without realizing that any manifestation of infection had started ten to fourteen days earlier.

The humble approach would have been to send a delegation of CDC workers to Wuhan to help the Chinese authorities contain the outbreak at its source. Unfortunately, the Chinese leaders weren't being honest about the extent of the virus, either, which prevented anyone from the CDC visiting that country.

That is supposedly what the CDC does. Such activities used to be a component of the National Security Council. A statement from the recent edition of VOX read:

> When Bolton became Trump's national security advisor in 2018, he moved quickly to disband the White House National Security Council's Di-

rectorate for Global Health Security and Biodefense, which President Barrack Obama set up after the 2014-2016 Ebola outbreak to lead federal coordination and preparation for disease outbreaks.

Trump, arrogantly obsessed with dismantling everything the Obama administration put in place, placed American lives at risk by abolishing the group that was set up based on lessons learned by early containment of the Ebola outbreak before it ever reached American shores.

Trump's missteps continued, most based on the rejection of any scientific facts that might make Trump look as if his decisions were ill-advised. Whether it was ordering too few early tests to underestimating the need for ICU beds or ventilators to overstating the possible efficacy of drugs to treat the infection, arrogance ruled the day.

There will be a shift, however, and we are beginning to see it. Just as we as individuals realize how little power we have over this virus and the extent of the worldwide pandemic, the government will realize its up against a powerful enemy, and lawmakers must do what they can in those areas they are able to control. If that occurs, and I believe it will and must for our survival, it will be due to the triumph of humility over arrogance. We will collectively invoke the Serenity Prayer, take into account the factors we can control, and do our best to optimize those. We will invoke the wisdom to know the difference between those things we can control and those we can't. Families are locked into their homes, doing what they can to keep each other safe, provide an environment conducive to education, suppress boredom, and promote family attachment. By controlling those factors within the walls of our homes and doing our best there, we can diminish the number of deaths.

The president and politicians everywhere will realize they must humbly accept the truth, no matter how grim, and tell it to their citizens, who will deal with it in some miraculous ways. We will rise up in innovative and compassionate ways to care for ourselves, our families, and those outside our homes with humility, empathy, and joy.

CHAPTER 8

Sufficiency and Humility

In the early stages of the coronavirus pandemic, my friend, the preacher, said, "God gives us just enough. Be the hope, and we are not alone." I heard him say that online, because all gatherings of people were cancelled and/or forbidden by public health officials.

The world has changed, possibly forever. Our daily routines while stuck at home, trying to feed and educate our children while remaining safe from the virus, are completely altered. For the first time since the nuclear arms race and the threatened Armageddon of the second half of the 20th century, we face a threat that could alter, if not completely eliminate, the human race.

When I heard him say those words, I realized our survival wasn't based on masks, social distancing, toilet paper, rice, beans, or how much hand sanitizer we had left. Those things are important for day-to-day existence, but for actual survival, we must have a mindset of humility, acceptance, tranquility, the knowledge we aren't alone, and knowing that the universe will give us just enough. We must also live in enough hope to understand where we are, why we're here, and what we need to do to combat that which threatens us.

We are challenged to find what we can do. When I hear of the many heroic doctors and nurses working in ER and ICU units throughout the world, I feel guilty and envious. Guilt strikes, because I no longer work in that arena, where I might do some good. Envy comes, because I wish I could be there at the time when all physicians are sorely needed.

I answered an online ad from New York's Governor Cuomo asking for doctors to come out of retirement and help them in their time of need, humbly knowing in my heart there was no way I could leave my family or even that I could physically or emotionally do such work anymore. I spoke to a dear, old friend, Dr. Friedman, who worked in an ICU unit in Chicago, after he came off a twenty-four-hour shift caring for ten patients of all ages who were extremely ill, intubated and living on ventilators, some in shock and unable to breathe, alone in their beds without family members to visit them.

Maybe I could communicate with those in the trenches, helping them express their frustrations and fears to someone who truly understood, who, in better times, also fretted over patients in my care who were in extreme conditions. I beat myself up over kids who died in my care, and I wondered what it felt like to lose tens or hundreds of people. The issue was too big for me to comprehend.

I humbly did what I could, caring for my family, preparing for the worst, and holding the hope that most of us would be all right. Many who have been infected with the coronavirus had mild or no symptoms. Their bodies produced antibodies for that virus, which, if isolated and prepared, could be administered to those who had the active disease. That might shorten the course of their illness and improve their symptoms and hopes for survival. It was humbling to know there was something we could do simply by surviving. Maybe that was the lesson.

We shouldn't increase our stress by worrying over the things we can't physically do. We must humbly accept whatever we can do and do it gracefully and thankfully, accepting with faith that we've been given just enough. We must also have hope to clear our minds of useless worry and clutter, making it possible to do those things that might help, each in our own way and own time. Most importantly, we must remember we aren't alone.

Cuomo vs. Trump

"The authority of the president is total."
Donald J. Trump, 4/13/20

One interesting ritual that developed during the pandemic was the President's Daily Briefing, or what I affectionately call, "The Trump Show." Each day, the president assembled a collection of experts from business and science to give an update on the status of the country's reaction to the corona virus outbreak. Unfortunately, before he finally accepted the word of the CDC doctors, warning him hundreds of thousands of Americans might die from the pandemic, he systematically lied to the public about everything, including the availability of testing, personal protective equipment, ventilators, and the possible death toll. Instead, he said, "Like a miracle, it will one day wash away."

He was never able to hold a briefing without congratulating himself and turning the focus on himself. On April 30, 2020, after he announced the need to continue safe distancing to reduce the number of potential deaths from 2.2 million to 100,000, he called it a great job! Then he spent a considerable amount of time complaining about his hair blowing in the wind while brushing it back and saying, "See what I put up with? This is my own hair."

In contrast, the traditional news media began broadcasting New York State Governor Andrew Cuomo's press briefings. Viewing a professional politician was a completely different experience than seeing President Trump, who was called by his real-estate mogul peers in New York, a "carnival barker."

Cuomo, a true leader, began with a clear statement of the facts, an impassioned list of the needs to better care for the residents of his state, and then he typically ended with an emotional/spiritual description of how the pandemic affected him and his family while making sure he mentioned the positive experience that might result from such a world-changing event.

There was never a clearer example of the leadership styles of arrogance (Trump) vs. humility (Cuomo). Interestingly, one factor that panicked Trump was the fact that Cuomo had more viewers and better ratings than himself. Trump, a product of reality TV, always gauges success by his TV ratings.

It was reassuring that the American public exhibited the humility to find less comfort in the hubris of the president than in the humility expressed by Governor Cuomo. He became America's governor. I live in Florida, where the governor was reluctant to suggest a stay-at-home order. It was reassuring and comforting to me to listen to Cuomo's wise words each day. During times when humility rules the day, what people need most is honesty, followed by authenticity. We don't need misinformation, bravado, and egocentricity.

In the future, when this story goes into the history books, we will learn that the arrogant Mr. Trump was the worst president in history, responsible for more deaths even than wartime presidents. Our hope is that a humble acceptance of the facts, our vulnerabilities, and an honest assessment of our assets and liabilities in defending ourselves, will save as many as possible. The principles of humility lead us to almost anyone but Trump.

Being Alive: Humbly Recognizing Humanity

As of April, 2020, when I wrote this, we're in the midst of the early stages of the pandemic, the "End of the beginning," as Winston Churchill once said. By the time this book is published, and people read it, we will either have survived or not.

Two things are certain. One is that we will have learned some important lessons, and the other is that we'll never be the same. While we're being forced to distance ourselves from each other, we must not lose sight of our fundamental need as human beings to connect. I have written about this previously, but I haven't yet reflected on the need to distance while connecting and the challenge that creates.

One of my favorite Broadway show tunes is by Sondheim and comes from the show *Company*. It was set to open a revival on Sondheim's ninetieth birthday in March, 2020, but Broadway went dark, so the opening was delayed until further notice.

Part of the lyrics of the song are:

> Someone you have to let in
> Someone whose feelings you spare
> Someone who, like it or not,
> Will want you to share
> A little, a lot....

That is the most-famous song in the musical about a guy whose friends throw him a surprise birthday party and try to convince him to get serious about meeting a woman and forming a relationship that might even lead to marriage. Robert, the main character, values his singleness and his three girlfriends, to whom he is not committed.

The song *Being Alive* is performed by Robert at the end of the second act. He has come to realize that being alone isn't all he thought. In the final verse are the words, "alone is not alive." He concludes that, as messy as intimacy and relationships can be, with people being too involved in someone else's life, keeping them awake worrying about their problems and driving them crazy, that is what humans are genetically programmed to do. To be intimate and be driven crazy by someone you love is the definition of humanity.

Earlier, I discussed the theories of attachment, which offer an academic explanation for why humans must humbly attach to one another to feel fulfilled and find joy in life. There is more to it, however. There is also the messy, crazy, heart-wrenching need to be connected that makes us human. It almost explains why people are compelled or driven to be connected. It takes humility to be able to commit to the imperfection of a human relationship, something we need as badly as oxygen to survive.

Governor Cuomo's response to the pandemic and devastation of so many lives in his state brought out his ability to lead by comforting others and doing his best to support helping. His brother, CNN anchor Chris Cuomo, contracted the virus and became quite ill, needing to quarantine himself in the basement of his family home. Governor Cuomo interviewed him during one of his press briefings.

"I feel horribly for those who go through this alone," Chris Cuomo said. "I'm lucky. I have a wife who loves me and provides everything for me. This illness knocks you down, and you can't do anything when the fever is there. All I have to do is sit down here and recover."

Alone is not alive. One tragic aspect of this illness is that if someone is sick enough to be admitted to a hospital, they must be admitted alone due to isolation policies. There is no one at their bedside to hold their hand, even when they're dying. Dying alone is one of the worst horrors of life.

To live, we must be connected. We can't do it alone. To connect, we must be humble, not arrogant, if we wish to inherit and be part of the universe of humanity.

We face an incredibly unique situation. In the midst of a global pandemic that is reaching historic proportions of death, the U.S. leads the world in deaths, mainly because we arrogantly ignored the epidemic while it enveloped countries over which we felt superior.

We are asked to distance ourselves socially, to be separate and yet apart. We're also expected to remain connected. We must, which means we have to resort to our own creativity. Thankfully, we have electronic telecommunications that enable us to converse across distances. People are also doing wonderful things, like gathering on their balconies and porches at seven o'clock, when shifts change, to cheer the healthcare workers who are on the front lines against the disease. We're in a war that we could possibly lose badly. I might not survive long enough to see the publication of this book, but, if I survive, I will cherish the love we felt when we were threatened by a submicroscopic killer that was smarter and more adaptable than we were.

When I go out of the house to walk the dog and get a little bit of exercise, I feel burdened by guilt that I'm too old and medically challenged to assist my brothers fighting in the trenches. I make eye contact with other frightened, isolated, possibly ill citizens also walking. We smile and nod if we're close enough, hoping we all survive. We are connected by our shared humanity, need for love, desire for connection, and our hope we will live long enough to touch our loved ones again, make love, laugh with our children, see another Christmas, dance at weddings, and offer love.

Pandemic of Arrogance, Survival by Humility

Since the pandemic began our response and that of our president have been classic examples of how arrogance not only separates us from one another, promoting divisions and alienation. It also potentially separates thousand from our lives. President Trump said, "One hundred thousand deaths would be a good job."

The worst of the arrogant separation occurred during the early phases of this period, as we saw hot spots of infection as being different from the rest of the world. Our country took longer to experience symptoms of COVID-19. As governors pleaded for supplies to save lives, they were criticized for not being prepared, yet it has long been the norm that, when there is a national crisis, we depend on the federal government, which is tasked with treating all states and citizens equally. That is a profoundly important American principle, which the current president mocks and belittles each time he treats states and countries as the "other." Someone once said, "Without borders, we have no country."

The reality of the virus is that it's more of an equal-opportunity actor than the leaders of the people it infects. North and south, urban and rural, rich and poor, educated and uneducated, Black or Brown or White, old and young, are artificially imposed, arrogant differentiations that mean nothing to the virus.

It's clear now, and it will become clearer after the pandemic finally clears, that arrogance led to the deaths of thousand, if not millions, of human beings. That is an important fact. The concept of regions might be helpful in a postmortem epidemiological study of the pandemic's progression, but in the midst of its early stages, as body bags are piling up, artificial separations forged by arrogance mean nothing.

If anything can save us, it will be embracing humility and the connections it brings. It's ironic that connection will save us, just at the time when we must socially distance even within our homes. There are signs humility is starting to take hold.

We sit it at the bedside of the sick and dying, where nurses hold the gloved hands of those they've never met before, because their families aren't allowed to be with them. Doctors and nurses have traveled from across the country to assist New York City, where medical staff are dying as fast as their patients.

Farmers, including undocumented immigrants, remain working in their fields so our grocery stores can remain open. We see humility in the unemployed domestic worker, also possibly undocumented, who takes a night job cleaning and disinfecting a local grocery store, so other people will be safe. We see it in the multitudes across the globe, who cheer and bang pots and pans for the healthcare workers out their windows to honor healthcare workers at the change of the hospital shift each evening.

Unfortunately, we won't see humility in us as a people when enough die so that we all know someone who has passed. Will our ultimate connection, and thus our humility, come only as we gasp for air at the end of our lives, longing to hold the hand of a loved one, or to feel the relief of having an endotracheal tube and ventilator after the supply has run out? I hope we accept the fact that humility is the only thing that will save us before it's too late.

After the Pandemic—the New Normal

Although we don't know when or how, the pandemic will end. When it does, we may have a renaissance unequaled since the one the followed the Middle Ages, which was also characterized by a plague.

Education and Business

We learned we can survive at home. The only risk seems to be that we might kill each other out of tedium and cabin fever. With our present technological capabilities, most of what we do in offices or classrooms can be done at home. Is the quality as good? Sometimes it is. Sometimes it isn't.

My daughter, trying to take classes at home, is disoriented by not having free access to a professor. Many people are like her. They need the structure of getting up, going to class each day, and studying for quizzes and tests to maintain discipline and incentive. Some, however, like the freedom of being able to progress at their own pace. The same applies to the workplace.

Trust Science

This situation has shown us that science and politics don't mix. When politicians make predictions about hard science, or worse, try to dabble in medicine and recommend medications and treatments that haven't been scientifically tested, needless loss of life can occur. The COVID-19 pandemic offered a glimpse of the juxtaposition of science and politics just when we needed it, right before the next election. We can make wiser decisions than in earlier years. Lives are truly at stake.

We Overconsume

**Shopping for
Home and Family Is Our Core**

families in a time of scarcity and diminished mobility due to social distancing made us realize how we buy more than we need. Over the years, we grew up planning for times of lack by buying more than we needed. That was wasteful. When we buy more than we need, not only do we keep it from others who might need it more, we don't use it, and it goes to waste. Even before the pandemic, Americans threw away vast amounts of food that could be used to feed the hungry and homeless.

We Can Sacrifice for the Greater Good

We can mobilize for the greater good. We have a strong sense of family, community, and country. We are primarily motivated by preserving our lives and those of our family. Thousands of healthcare workers volunteered to work in hospitals far from home, putting their lives at risk, to help where they were needed. Despite arguments over what distance policy is and what jurisdiction makes the rules, people are practicing social distancing, wearing masks in public, and leaving home only for essential services.

Healthcare workers face an illness the likes of which none have seen before. My dear friend, an adult pulmonologist and intensive-care physician, who is still practicing after forty years, describes it as like nothing he has seen. The stricken who have respiratory disease, decompensate incredibly fast and often end up intubated. Once intubated and placed on ventilators, those in New York hospitals face an eighty-percent chance of dying. If they survive being placed on a ventilator, they remain there for weeks. Worse, they are alone, with only healthcare workers, such as physicians, nurses, and respiratory therapists, to hold their hands as they heal or die.

Like soldiers going into battle, those healthcare workers put on their gowns each day and walk into their hospitals facing devastating critical illness and possible death for themselves and their families. They do it without question, offering their potential sacrifice to a strong sense of duty, and, above all, to patients they don't know.

We're staying home during the pandemic, as we should. We work and study online and telephonically. My wife does the shopping, which was usually my job, trying to protect me as well as the public I might meet. I am high risk due to my age, weight, heart disease, high blood pressure, diabetes, and metabolic syndrome. It's a strange time that lacks the normal rituals of life. When should we get up? When should we do laundry? Why bother cleaning the house if we'll just mess it up again? If there is an economic shutdown, why is there so much food in the freezer that we can barely close the door?

As I prepared a drink for myself the other night and a glass of wine for my wife, I grabbed an iced tea for our daughter and prepared to catch up on an old episode of *Gilmore Girls*. It was a beautiful moment, a gift. We were together for a short time and still healthy enough to grasp our core of family.

We all have moody moments, and I admit to being grumpy at times, but overall, I felt joyful to share those moments with the ones I loved. We might never have that opportunity again. As family members, it is our fundamental duty to keep each other safe, love one another, and be together. Once the pandemic is over, I hope we don't lose what we gained from such an odd gift.

We Love Arts & Sports

The first big blow to sports was the loss of the NBA playoffs and the NCAA basketball tournament. Then came the delayed MLB season, no tennis, and no golf. Next will probably be the NFL and quite likely the cancellation of the Superbowl in early 2021, which was to be held in my beloved Tampa!

Perhaps worse, and more heartfelt for me, was the closing of Broadway and the theater season, just as the industry was preparing for the Tony Awards. These things are our life blood. We need science to define life and explain, but we need the arts to celebrate life and articulate our human experience. I believe the things we utilize to celebrate life will be preserved. It's up to us, and we'll bring them back, because we need them.

They will come back in different forms, but it's difficult to imagine sporting events without roaring crowds or a superb musical without a standing ovation. It might be that way for a while, though.

Once thing is certain—if we survive this, we'll have a new appreciation for life and its gifts. Nothing celebrates life and human achievement like sports and the arts. We will hopefully humbly, meekly realize how quickly we can lose the things that make life worth living. They will return, and we will humbly accept whatever form they take, although not without some grumbling and lamenting of the old days. That happens, anyway. You can hear it at any sports bar, but don't go there until they are safe to reopen.

We Will Open to a New Normal

People ask when life will return to "normal." Dr. Anthony Fauci, certainly a hero in the pandemic information story, told us on April 6, 2020, that if we call normal what the world looked like before the virus hit, without a vaccine and antibody testing, we may never return to prepandemic normal.

I optimistically expect that we'll accept a postpandemic reality whatever it is. People accepted tremendous changes in society after the Great Depression, the two World Wars, 9/11, and the Great Recession. We adapt, accept, and humbly appreciate the fundamentals of who we are and where we've been.

This is difficult to see when there are thousands of people dying in emergency rooms, ICUs, and bedrooms around the world, but the sun will shine again. We will laugh and cry together at family gatherings, celebrate our children's milestones, marvel at our resilience, and celebrate how adversity results in growth and positive change.

Forgiveness, Redemption, and Hope

Positivity and humility are the characteristics that will pull us through and render us equipped to handle the new normal in the most-productive, rewarding ways. The slights and hurts we felt before the pandemic will pale in significance once we survive. We will have a new perspective, the benefits of which will allow us to move past things that are no longer important. Humility will bring that perspective, with the result of uniting and connecting us. Arrogance will feed our egos to think the insignificant, personal struggles we experienced before the pandemic are still important and the focus of our lives. Bringing those damaged slights forward will only separate us and disconnect us as a time when we most need connection.

The best way to maintain hope is be exercising gratitude. One very practical tool for his comes from Oprah. Each day, she writes down in her gratitude journal five things from the previous day she feels thankful for. It could include people, experiences, thoughts, emotions, foods, movies, and books. That puts into perspective the good things in our lives and demonstrates we will continue to have things to be thankful for each day.

It we put into action another principle espoused in this book, that even negative events in our lives are gifts for which we should be thankful, it becomes easy to see how our five things to be grateful for, which my wife calls "thanks you fors," will be easy to list each day. As the list grows, so does our hope that better times are ahead, and miracles abound around us every day.

Plans Are Not Paths

I have one daughter who is a young doctor at the beginning of a hopefully long career, but her career path and academic position in New York may be changed forever. My other daughter is in college, although she had to continue her studies from home, and also wants to be in medicine. Her plan involves passing organic chemistry and getting accepted into medical or PA school, but due to the pandemic, her pathway in life has become uncertain.

What can we do beyond accepting that we must have the humility to choose between paths that are presented to us, knowing we may not understand the pathways of our life journey until they are upon us? I'm happy they both chose medicine. With the heroism of the doctors, nurses, and medical personnel in hospitals around the world, medical professionals are perhaps the most-admired people in the world right now. They will do well and have long, happy lives, but those lives might not resemble what they imagined, whether they work in a hospital or an outpatient setting in a large city or small town.

Both daughters have come to realize that all bets are off. I hope they remember to be open to the possibilities of what might lie ahead. Some arrogant people feel they can control the trajectory of their lives. My daughters vacillate between arrogance and humility. I hope they settle on humility and accept the life that comes to them. Both have very humane, compassionate personalities. Of course, both are brilliant and will do well.

I'm afraid the younger one trends toward the arrogant side of thinking she failed if she didn't follow the path she envisioned from middle school through high school. Humility dictates that she must accept her failures as gifts leading to her life's true purpose. That can be a tough lesson for young people growing up in the midst of a pandemic, but I hope they can learn and appreciate it.

Elections Matter

During his 2016 campaign, Trump said, "I alone can do it!" He also said, "I could shoot a person on Fifth Avenue and get away with it." Lately, he asked, "Did you know I'm number one on Facebook?" Worst of all, when asked by a member of the press if he takes responsibility for the COVID-19 testing fiasco, he replied, "I take no responsibility."

When this is over, we will see that the devastation, death, and suffering of Americans and others around the world are a direct result of this president's arrogance, dishonesty, and egocentricity. With the current election, we have a clear choice between arrogance (Trump) and humility (nearly anyone else).

PART SIX

LESSONS FOR LIVING HUMBLY

CHAPTER 9

Although I'd been chipping away at the idea for this book for a while, I finally began writing in 2016 when I was inspired by the increased arrogance I saw in American society. I saw the rise of Donald Trump's popularity as a symptom, not the disease. Then he became president, and the book seemed to write itself. With the global coronavirus pandemic, the life-threatening effects of arrogance became clear.

I have tried to make the point that our only hope in this era is through connection, possible even in a time of social distancing, which we can achieve by living humbly and meekly. Through such a meek, humble connection we can inherit the earth. I have tried to describe how that looks in many aspects of life from education to politics to religion and to relationships. In offering some of the essential humility lessons to be learned from the pandemic, I have presented practical considerations of humility over arrogance.

People will still want to know how to utilize these important principles day-to-day. I have created a list of daily humility practices. These are just suggestions on ways to face the day humbly, making it easier to connect and knowing that we are better and stronger when we are together, not divided.

Wake Ups with a Gratitude Prayer or Keep a Journal

One of my heroes is the late, great Wayne Dyer, a philosopher and author, who told his followers the best, most-essential, most-effective prayer was to say, "Thank you." He started each day with that the moment his feet touched the floor. I have related how Oprah writes in her journal five things each day she feels thankful for. Such things humble us, bring us hope, and help us live in awareness and be more mindful.

If you can, take five or ten minutes after waking, maybe with your first cup of coffee, to be thankful for what and who you have, for all the good in your life. That can be done seated or as you walk through the woods or down your neighborhood streets. I call that version "mobile meditation."

Take a Walk, Embrace Nature

It *is* possible to meditate while being mobile, although it's probably easier to be mindful and in the present without earphones, music, news, or podcasts. If that helps, though, people can try it, but you need to be mindful of what your senses experience as you walk. Take in the sights, smells, and sounds, which help you be mindful, and humbly accept the miracle of just being alive, the primary thing to be thankful for.

My dear, late father, who passed away in the midst of Hurricane Irma, as it tore up Florida's spine, was descending into the ravages of Parkinson's and dementia when a nurse asked him to write a sentence as part of a lengthy mental-status exam. He tentatively took the pencil, seeming to be fearful of what he might write, and put it to the paper to write, *I am alive.* A tear ran down his cheek, and I cried, too.

At that moment, he was thankful for the basic fact that he was still breathing and alive. He didn't need to take a walk outside to know that. He couldn't do that anymore, but he was mindful of his life, how he treasured it, and how he wanted to hang onto it. It was a beautiful moment, and I recall it often, particularly in light of the pandemic, with so many people dying alone, fearing to lose that for which they are most thankful.

Eat a Healthy Breakfast and Remember the Alive Five

Restaurants are closed and may still be that way by the time someone reads this book. There is no end in sight for the stay-at-home order. We shop and eat at home, making it the perfect opportunity to reinforce or discover healthy eating. In the *Alive Five*, I promoted the idea of family meals, which have been shown to prevent many problems for kids and parents, including obesity, truancy, drug abuse, eating disorders, and even teen pregnancy. By eating together, a family has the change to get to know each other better and actually have conversation. Emphasizing fruits and vegetables is workable as long as the supply trucks keep running. Farmers and food producers are as much our heroes as first responders.

It might be difficult to avoid sugar, because it's natural to gain weight from comfort food when locked in our houses. Comfort foods are usually laden with high-fructose corn syrup. Knowing what we eat, along with other mindfulness techniques, are possible during the pandemic, so why not do them?

Connect with Your Family Early and Often

Once life returns to a semblance of normal, and it will, it's important to stay connected with family, especially with one's significant other. Spouses are the witnesses to your life, evidence of your existence and purpose, the one person with whom you can be vulnerable. They know your strengths and weaknesses sometimes better than you do.

While we were cooped up with the kids during the stay-at-home order, responsibilities were clear and duties were well-defined. We acted as the protectors of our family and ourselves. It wasn't easy, and sometimes tension reached the boiling point, but we tried to remain civil and kind even if we didn't always succeed. Other than walking the dog or taking a solo walk around the block while listening to music, there wasn't much escape from tension. Being forced to deal with it in a fair, controlled way was a valuable lesson that will hopefully continue after the pandemic ends.

We have teens in our family, and sometimes, I forget the dicta I tell others when dealing with adolescents. The most-effective way to talk to them is to listen. Teens need to be seen, heard, and know they matter. When they are hurt, angry, or offended, my kids shut down, usually right after exploding at their mother or me. In that scenario, the worst thing to do is try to force them out of their shells. The best thing to do in almost every situation dealing with teens is to wait it out, stay available to them, listen on their terms and in their time. That is the respect they need, crave, and deserve.

Walk in the Shoes of Others before Judging

One of the clearest examples of humble living is our approach to those we deal with every day. Once we are freed from our home-based quarantine, we'll be back in the workforce, the office, or factories, and we will also go shopping. We will go out to restaurants, bars, coffee shops, movies, theaters, and sporting events. Hopefully, we can use the skills we developed while cooped up with our families when dealing with the outside world again.

When confronted by others, we should listen humbly to their point of view. People are often motivated by the desire to be right, not necessarily doing the right or kind thing. If someone is in an adversarial profession like law enforcement or legal consultation, it's his job to convince the adversary he is right. In that case, an effective strategy may be to recognize the point of view of the other and its genesis. Most of us have conflicts with people when it isn't your job to convince them of our point of view. Once we acknowledge the point of view of someone with whom we are in conflict, that will often defuse the situation.

Your being right isn't as important as you might think. It's only our egos that tell us such things. Once we humbly acknowledge others, we can connect with them. With each person we establish a connection, we come a little closer to inheriting the earth.

All of us should try to set our egos aside and let the other person have a different point of view and share it with us. Once we acknowledge that point of view, it is surprising how quickly connection and peace results. That should not be considered weakness in Trumpian terms. It takes great strength to set one's ego aside and value another's point of view. Humility takes strength, not frailty.

Governor Cuomo often said that real strength also means having the ability to show love to others. That is strong advice.

Humbly Engage with Your News Source

During the pandemic home isolation, I stared at the TV, usually MSNBC but also local news. One phenomenon that occurred was that a person's reality is affected by that person's source of news. People watching Fox News were later to get on board with even the existence of the coronavirus infection and the seriousness of the impending pandemic, while those who watched MSNBC tended to be skewed toward viewing it as a serious disease with a high death rate. It's important to fact check everyone, humbly accepting that even a favorite news source and the personalities with whom we grow attached may not get it right. To be humble in this case means to be smart and circumspect in order to be armed with information that will better equip you to care for yourself and your family.

There is a survival aspect to humility. It is clear that arrogance, as shown by President Trump and his followers, is literally killing people. Even in the depths of the pandemic, Trump arrogantly pushed treatments in which he had a financial interest, like hydrocholorquine. We are lucky to have the Internet and look for the raw data from which any intelligent, humble person can learn and draw conclusions. The CDC website is a perfect example. After the pandemic clears, we'll have an election, unless something goes terribly wrong.

Use Social Media to Truly Connect

As physicians who aren't on the front line due to health and personal reasons, my wife and I tried to continue teaching and sharing our experiences through Facebook and YouTube posts. In ancient Greek, *doctor* means the same as *teacher*. Through our reflections and experiences with sick children, we can help people through the pandemic, including times before it started and after it is over. We help them live their best, healthiest lives. It is another avenue through which we can explore and incorporate telemedicine, which may become the norm after being used by so many.

Embrace Mindfulness

The fifth element of the *Alive Five* is perhaps my favorite—the mindfulness movement espoused by Deepak Chopra and others. This movement has become popular and may be one factor that turns the wellness movement around to help us take charge of our own well-being. Awareness of one's essential, spiritual self is a result of humbly accepting living in the moment. Multitasking is no longer considered a virtue. When one performs multiple tasks simultaneously, they rarely do all of them well. To be humble is to pay attention to where one is emotionally, spiritually, and physically. More than that, humility means accepting where we are in those realms and working from there.

As we move through the day, whether it's at home in quarantine, at work in an office, calling the hospital taking care of sick babies, or retired and reading a good book, we should do a deep-breathing exercise as a mini-meditation. We should stop and take stock of our surroundings, give thanks and appreciation, note our feelings, and, if it helps, write them down, then move on in a spirit of gratitude and joy.

Recognize the Gifts in Your Family and Friends and Tell Them

Greet your family with joy and gratitude each morning with the most good will you can muster, even when you don't feel like it. You can feel grateful even if life isn't perfect. This is truly a "Fake it till you make it" experience. I don't mean to suggest being fake. Deep in our hearts, we can always find a grain of gratitude for family, even when they make us crazy. I suggest we humbly put aside our ego, filled with petty hurts and jealousies, and embrace the grateful portion of our psyches and express it.

If we do that with each encounter throughout the day, connections will grow, and so will gratitude. We need to embrace the grateful parts of our relationships with all, express them, and find ourselves experiencing a more-joyful day. There will be times when others get on our nerves in any family situation, especially when it's aggravated by the prolonged lockdown. Be aware of those triggers and avoid them. When I feel myself losing control, I take a short walk or retreat to the bedroom and bathroom, practicing another form of social distancing.

Do Something Creative Each Day

We discovered this during the stay-at-home order. My wife returned to her painting, and I finished this book, working on getting my novel finally published, and went back to playing piano as often as I could. Art and creativity are essential to appreciation and interpretation of life on our planet.

Accept the Fallibility of Being Human for Yourself and Others

Human beings are far from perfect. We make mistakes regularly. It happens, because we're human, so we must practice humble forgiveness. When our kids do stupid things, which they will, we shouldn't scream, holler, or, even worse, call them demeaning names. Recognize the goodness in their hearts, continue loving them, and forgive them. This requires humility. There may be in no better way to connect with others. Humility dictates that we not suffer slights, hold grudges, or seek retribution for perceived wrongs.

Acknowledge Miracles—Watch for Feathers

In our mindfulness practice, we must recognize some fundamental truths. Each experience in our lives, no matter how negative it is on its face, is a gift that will teach us something or help us make a necessary course correction in our lives. Miracles, like feathers, are all around. We notice and appreciate them only if we open our eyes, become aware, and see them. This is connected with being mindful, appreciative, and filled with forgiveness.

In the End, only Kindness Matters

A direct quote from the Jewel song *Hands*, and it's true, is that kindness is at the core of humility and connectedness. It's necessary for us to attach humbly. There's no need to go too far out of our way. The possibilities for random acts of kindness, like feathers and miracles, are all around us and present themselves each day. We should choose kindness, do the nice thing, and take the generous route. As my very Southern ex-mother-in-law admonished her children, "Be sweet!" Kindness connects. When practiced randomly, it humbles us.

Live Life as a Spiritual Being Having a Human Experience, not Vice Versa

No matter what someone's religious or political traditions are, we should live as a spiritual being inhabiting a physical body, not the other way around. When our spirituality, rather than our physicality, is the focus of our everyday activities and choices, we will naturally connect and treat each other humbly. That allows us to put our own mortality into perspective. We must humbly accept the fact that we will die, and there's nothing we can do about it. This attitude is expressed in the *Serenity Prayer*. Mindfully living our spiritual lives allows us to grasp the concept of eternity, which exists somewhere between our thoughts and our breaths. That will certainly humble us.

Live the Serenity Prayer

Choosing to live humbly is related to the *Serenity Prayer*—the concept that we should try to change what we can, accept things in life we can't change, and pray to know the difference between them. This takes humility, mindfulness, and the ability to forgive oneself. If we humbly face each challenge, event, and individual who comes into our sphere of influence with the idea of serenity, we will experience less frustration, more success, and more peace. That is the whole purpose of humility.

The Triple Threat Pandemic: Actually, There Are Four

We are in the midst of an historic moment. For those of us who aren't as mindful as the psychologists and spiritual teachers tell us we should be, we sometimes don't recognize these historic periods for what they are until they have passed. We can be so busy dealing with the personal and family impacts of current events that we don't have the opportunity to take a breath, look around, and take stock of our situation.

When we take that moment, it doesn't take any extraordinary awareness to realize we're in the midst of an ongoing killer pandemic. The resulting economic crisis will take years to resolve, and racial tensions are coming to an historic but necessary climax. Those make up what I call the Triple Threat, but there is a fourth item—the arrogance of the president and his administration. That factor makes the first three items far worse and more threatening to the existence of our democracy, and, possibly, our civilization.

As I write this article, there are more than 2 million COVID-19 cases in the U.S. and over 110,000 deaths. Reports from the front lines tell us how horrible those deaths are. Short of a useful treatment and a workable vaccine, there is no end in sight. Despite that, we continue to open the economy by promoting events and locations that put people in close proximity, spreading the virus with its associated suffering and death. Humility would tell us to be judicious about opening certain businesses and activities, yet the president tells us there are so many cases, because we're doing so many tests. If we stop testing, he says, there would be few if any cases. The recklessness and inhumanity of that arrogance is astounding.

Concerning the economic recession and depression resulting from necessarily closing our economy due to the virus, the president tells us that we need to open up and get the economy moving. If we don't, people will lose their livelihoods and then kill themselves. He claims that is the true mortality risk from the pandemic.

He points to the artificially rising stock market as evidence of the vitality and optimism of the economy. I am not sophisticated enough to explain that economic disconnect, but I know that the stock market doesn't necessarily reflect what's actually happening in the economy. People are suffering from a combination of illness and economic collapse. Humility tells us to go slowly, be careful, and close certain elements of the economy again if spikes of the virus occur. The arrogance of our president is astonishing. He tells us to go out, spend money, open businesses, and just deal with the risks.

The third leg of the pandemic is the reality of systemic racism, which has always been there, but now has been brought to everyone's attention by the video evidence of George Floyd's murder, along with the deaths of others, like the unnecessary police shooting in Atlanta. Humility dictates that we finally accept that all of us are human, regardless of race, and people deserve equal treatment and opportunity.

Our arrogant, all-powerful president has said that the MAGA members love Black people, and we must have "law and order." Those words invoke our racist past. Such a statement reflects our unmistakable and fundamental racism.

The pandemic will eventually pass, the economy will recover, and we will learn, change, and become fairer when we recognize the truth that Black lives really do matter. If we overcome the Triple Threat, it will only be because our humility overcomes the Fourth Threat—the administration's systemic arrogance. If not contained, that arrogance could slow or disrupt any advances we make as a people.

EPILOGUE

Viral Humility—Final Thoughts on the Pandemic 4/9/20

At the time of this writing, our family is nearly one month into our stay-at-home quarantine. We've done a pretty good job. There are five of us, if I count Snickers the Wonder Dog. We stay inside except to walk Snickers, take a few short walks around the neighborhood, and go to the grocery store. We used to visit the grocery store every day, but we have cut that to twice a week.

Our work has mainly been at home, mine as a writer and consultant, my wife as an artist. Our kids are students who work online at home. Our daughter was sent home from college in another state, and our high-school son, who is subject to shared custody between his mother and father, goes back and forth every few days. Luckily, both places are in the same part of town, so the trip is quick and easy.

As a retired physician, I am extremely fortunate. My income is mainly fixed, so I don't have to worry too much about that. My 401K has seen quite a roller coaster ride, though.

This week is Holy Week. We aren't the most-religious family in town, but we have gone to church most weeks. For many years, we attended both the Maundy Thursday and Good Friday services, along with the most-glorious service of the year, Sunrise Easter Service at the water's edge. For this year, attendance will be, like it has been recently, online.

That's not so bad. We have plenty to be thankful for. We have a comfortable, air-conditioned home, plenty of food, and even enough toilet paper. Still, stress and worry are pronounced. Why?

"What we fear most is that which we do not understand." That dictum is often stated by physicians, teachers, parents, and philosophers. We are starved for information, something solid we can plan on for the future, something to reassure knowledgeable, aware children.

The president's daily briefing has become nothing more than an entertainment show. We learn more from the briefings of governors from states not our own. We follow the CDC directives. We've learned the mechanics of grocery deliveries to enable us to remain home even more. However, we have no idea how long we'll have to do this, to keep suspending the lives we once knew.

Each morning as I lay in bed, as the oldest, least-healthy member of our family, I perform my own symptom assessment. I'm at the age where vague symptoms like aches and pains, weird breathing patterns, and daily stuffy nose from hay fever are common. I ask myself, *Do I have a fever today? Does my chest feel tight? What does that cough mean? Why am I so tired this morning? Why do I feel so sad and depressed?*

I try to contact old friends, those who are older and have kids scattered across the country. One of those is on the front lines in a major U.S. city, a physician caring for the sickest patients he has seen in forty years of practice. He is constantly impressed by the fact that they stay sick for so long, then die. He and his colleagues are exhausted, worried not just about the health of their patients but also for themselves and their families. I'm at home, free of the virus, in a climate-controlled setting in an affluent neighborhood, and I worry about the unknown while feeling guilty that I'm unable to assist in the battle.

Commercials on the TV, which is almost always on, tell us this will eventually end, and I suppose it will. People say we will be better, stronger, and smarter afterward, but who knows? What will be left of the economy and our beloved institutions of sports, movies, theater, and medicine? I feel humbled by our vulnerability to a microbe but still remain hopeful that the beauty of the human spirit will bring us back.

It's not a time for arrogance, thinking we can control something we can't. It's a time for meekness, to affect what we can in our hearts and within the walls of our homes. If we love one another, follow the directives of science and not politicians, take a moment each day to give thanks, and use only as much toilet paper as we need, we will be fine...I think.

> The Serenity Prayer
> God, give me grace to accept with serenity
> The things that cannot be changed,
> Courage to change the things
> Which should be changed,
> And the wisdom to distinguish
> The one from the other.
> Living one day at a time,
> Enjoying one moment at a time,
> Accepting hardship as a pathway to peace,
> Taking, as Jesus did,
> This sinful world as it is,
> Not as I would have it,
> Trusting that You will make all things right,
> If I surrender to Your will,
> So that I may be reasonably happy in this life,
> And supremely happy with You forever in the next.
> Amen.
> Reinhold Niebuhr

The Prayer of St. Francis

Lord, make me an instrument of Your peace

Where there is hatred, let me sow love

Where there is injury, pardon

Where there is doubt, faith

Where there is despair, hope

Where there is darkness, light

And where there is sadness, joy.

O Divine Master, grant that I may

Not so much seek to be consoled as to console

To be understood, as to understand

To be loved, as to love

For it is in giving that we receive

And it's in pardoning that we are pardoned

And it's in dying that we are born to Eternal Life

Amen

www.ingramcontent.com/pod-product-compliance
Lightning Source LLC
Chambersburg PA
CBHW071516080526
44588CB00011B/1444